The Modern Practical Bread Baker

*Giving the Newest Methods of Making
Bread By Hand and Machinery*

by

Robert Wells

APPLEWOOD BOOKS
Bedford, Massachusetts

The Modern Practical Bread Baker

was originally published in

1900

ISBN: 978-1-4290-1253-9

Thank you for purchasing an Applewood book.
Applewood reprints America's lively classics—
books from the past that are still of interest
to the modern reader.
For a free copy of
a catalog of our
bestselling
books,
write
to us at:
Applewood Books
Box 365
Bedford, MA 01730
or visit us on the web at:
For cookbooks: foodsville.com
For our complete catalog: awb.com

Prepared for publishing by HP

ROBERT WELLS.

THE MODERN

PRACTICAL

BREAD BAKER:

GIVING

THE NEWEST METHODS OF MAKING BREAD
BY HAND AND MACHINERY;

ALSO

NEW IDEAS AND INSTRUCTIONS ON THE TRADE

With Appendix.

BY

ROBERT WELLS

AUTHOR OF

'The Bread and Biscuit Baker, and Sugar Boiler's Assistant";
"The Pastrycook and Confectioner's Guide," etc.

MANCHESTER:
ABEL HEYWOOD & SON, 56 & 58 OLDHAM-ST.
LONDON:
SIMPKIN, MARSHALL, HAMILTON, KENT, ADAMS, & CO.,'LIMITED,
STATIONERS' HALL COURT.

PREFACE.

Probably there are few callings that can claim an older or more respectable origin than that of the Baking Trade, and nothing marks the progress of the world's *cuisine* more clearly than the difference that exists between ancient and modern bread-making. It is interesting to note the change. The earliest method was to soak the grain in water and to dry it by natural or artificial heat, after having subjected it to pressure. The next advance was to pound or bray the grains in a mortar, or between stones; hence the word bread—*brayed*.

The oat-cakes of Scotland are prepared from grains that have been ground somewhat more thoroughly, and mixed with salt and water, kneaded and rolled out thin, and cooked before a good fire or on an iron girdle hung above the fire. Scones and pea meal bannocks are made in the same way. The Passover cakes of the Israelites are similarly prepared. The Southern hoe cake does not differ materially from the above varieties, which are all called unleavened, no leaven being used in their manufacture. Leaven is literally that which is applied internally to raise the bread, and it was first used by the Egyptians—presumably in the time of Moses. From the Egyptians it spread to the Greeks, then to the Romans, and from them to all parts of the world.

The baking industry (or the baking trade, as it is commonly called) has a deeper and fuller interest to mankind than any of its offshoots—pastry, confectionery, etc., as the one is a necessity and the others only luxuries. The staff of life, let it be made by man or woman, requires to be properly manipulated. This is of the most paramount interest, and assuredly goes to at once build up the wealth and stamina of a nation.

CONTENTS.

FLOUR:
    Chemical Examination of Flour 3
    Spiced Flour 5

ON YEASTS AND BARMS:
    Parisian Barm 7
    Sour Parisian Barm... 9
    On Bringing Away Parisian Barm without any previously-made Barm being mixed with the freshly-made liquid ... 9
    Virgin Barm 10
    Malt and Hop Barm 10
    Store 11
    American Patent Yeast 12
    Brewers' Barm 13
    German Yeast 13
    Scotch Yeast 14
    French Yeast 14
    English Compressed Yeast 14
    Compressed Yeasts when Stale and Unfit for Use 15
    How to Keep Yeasts Pure 17
    Leaven 17

SALT 18

WATER 19

FERMENTATION 20

SPONGING:
    Sunday Sponging 26
    On Increasing and Decreasing Sponges 28
    Sourness in Bread 29
    Unripe Sponges 32
    Flour Ferments... 33

CONTENTS.

SPONGING—*Continued.*

Quarter Sponges to take up one Sack of Flour... 34
Modern Method of Sponging... 35
Quick or Flying Sponges ... 36
Overnight Sponging in Large Firms ... 37
To make a Full Sponge with Parisian Barm without Quarter or Ferment... 37
How to Set a Sponge ... 37
How to treat Over-wrought Sponges ... 38

THE MANIPULATION OF DOUGH :

How to Make Dough by Hand ... 39
Method of Cutting Dough ... 40
How to Weigh-off a Batch of Bread ... 41
How to Roll-up Loaves of Dough... 42
How to Mould a Square Loaf ... 43
How to Mould a Round Loaf... 44
Moulding and Boarding ... 44
Setting or Running Batches ... 46

PLAIN AND FANCY BREAD, ETC. :

Vienna Bread ... 50
Fancy Cottage Loaves ... 50
How to make Twists ... 51
Coburgs, or Cobs ... 51
Common Vienna Loaves... 52
Melvin Loaves ... 52
Sandwich Loaves ... 53
French Loaves ... 53
Box Rolls... 53
Pulled Bread ... 54
Soda Bread... 54
Aerated Bread ... 54
Patent, or Unleavened Bread... 55
Home-made Bread ... 55
Family, or Home-baked Bread, made with Brewers' Barm ... 56
Names of Various Loaves made in Britain... 56
Hot Rolls in England ... 57
Scotch Rolls ... 58
Plain Round Rolls ... 59
Baps ... 59

CONTENTS. vii.

BROWN BREAD, WHEAT MEAL, RYE, ETC.
Wheat-meal Bread 61
Rye Bread 62
Brown-bread Meal 63
Maslen Bread 63
Aerated Malt Bread 64
Fermented Malt Bread 64
Germ Bread 65
Diet, or Wheat-meal Bread, Unfermented 65

SUBSTITUTES FOR WHEAT BREAD:
Bread made from Roots 67
Apple Bread 67
Meslin Bread 68
Ragwort Bread 68
Turnip Bread 68
Salep Bread 59
Oat and Barley Bread 69
Debretzen Bread 70
Bread a Hundred Years Old 70

OVENS:
Waggon Ovens 72
Furnace Ovens 74
Scotch Ovens 74
Various Other Ovens 76

GENERAL DETAILS:
The Ventilation of Bakehouses 77
The Effect of Cold or Chilled Dough on the Heat of an Oven.. 78
Heating New Ovens 79
Seasoning Bread Tins 79
How to Use up Old Bread 79
How to Ascertain the Heat of Water 80
A Standard for Bread 80
On Carrying Flour 81

MACHINERY, TOOLS, ETC.:
Pyrometers 83
Utensils Required for a Modern Bakery 83

ADULTERATION:
Alum, Potatoes, etc 87

APPENDIX:

Baking and Bakers in the Time of the Romans	94
The Foreign Element in London	99
Journeyman Bakers in London	100
Journeyman Bakers in Glasgow	102
Federation	105
Statistics of American & Canadian Bakers and Confectioners	105
Inefficient Workmen	106
Old Customs of the Trade	108
A Canny Scot	112
Scientific Views on Fermentative Physiology	113
The Properties of Starch	124
Dryness of Bread made from Roller-ground Flour	125
The Causes of Holes in Bread	128
Personal Cleanliness, etc.	130
An Appeal to the Trade	131
Concluding Remarks	132

THE MODERN PRACTICAL BREAD BAKER.

FLOUR.

Flour being one of the primary substances used in the manufacture of bread, and its good or bad qualities having everything to do with the bread baker's failure or success, I propose to treat of it in the first instance, and make it, as it were, my starting-point or foundation on which to raise the structure of my experiences.

In the buying of flour a modern baker should be a thorough expert. He should be capable of using his own practical judgment; judgment, too, of no mean order, but based on past experience. No man should buy a hundred sacks of flour at less than market value without first ascertaining its quality and condition. To buy cheaply is a good point, but to buy well is a better. Mr. Thoms, of Alyth, and Professor Jago have each invented an apparatus for testing flour, both of which are very easily understood and are of considerable value to the trade. Of course, the surest way of testing flour is by setting a sponge and baking a small quantity of bread from it; but the baker or buyer may form a pretty accurate idea of its quality by pressing a portion of the flour between the thumb and forefinger, and at the same time rubbing it gently in the hand for the purpose of making a level surface on the flour. If the flour feels loose and lively in the hand it may be supposed to be of good quality; but if it feels dead, damp, or clammy it is decidedly bad. Or take a watch with a smooth back and press it firmly upon the flour; by this means its colour may be ascertained by observing the pressed or smooth surface. If the flour be fine and white it may be considered good so far as colour goes; if brown, it shows that it is either made from inferior wheat or has been coarsely dressed. Brown flour, however, may be of good quality, and fine white flour may not; and bakers ought not to forget that flour should be kept a short time before being made into bread.

Flour's colour and appearance have been the most important factors in producing the recent revolutions in milling methods. Even those millers who believed that stone-milled flour made sweeter and better flavoured bread have gradually adopted roller-milled flour in its place. The reason of this is that bread made from roller-milled flour has a richer and better appearance.

Anyone watching the transactions between buyers and sellers at any of our leading corn markets will notice that one of the most frequent tests made is to place flours side by side and smooth their surfaces with a spatula, in order to show the relative qualities of colour. This test is familiar to nearly all millers and bakers, for it is doubtful whether there is a more fruitful source of dispute between them than colour. A parcel of flour is, perhaps, bought for forward delivery, and is taken from the miller in instalments. Most likely the first instalment is in every way equal to the sample from which the purchase was made, but after a while, as successive lots come in, differences are observed between the first and last received. As time goes on, the miller perhaps alters his mixture, and finds considerable difficulty in keeping his flour at a constant standard of colour. This is a difficulty everywhere, even when the same variety of wheat is being used. The sole remedy is close care and watchfulness.

In the larger mills samples of flour are tested and examined several times a day for colour and other properties. In order to explain discrepancies between bulk and sample, the theory of bleaching is commonly resorted to. That is to say, the sample apparently grows whiter by keeping, and thus presents a different appearance from the bulk. It is, however, more than doubtful whether this is a sufficient explanation in the majority of instances where a dispute has arisen on this matter of colour.

CHEMICAL EXAMINATION OF FLOUR.

This is really not millers' work, nor that of the merchant, but should be done by well-educated scientific chemists, as is commonly the case in France, where science and industry go hand in hand and mutually aid each other. By an examination so conducted, the limits of water, starch, gluten, and ashes are determined. The water contents of flour are easily ascertained by drying out a small quantity in an air-bath, at a temperature of 110° or 120° C. The driest flour contains six per cent. of water, while in some instances it will be found to contain as much as 25 per cent. The properties of starch and gluten are determined by separating one from the other. Tie the flour up in a small linen bag and knead it under water until the gluten has formed into a mass, which, if the flour is of poor quality, it will not do for a long time. In the water in which the flour is thus kneaded the starch will be found, and will very shortly settle at the bottom. Cerealin and casein, both nourishing nitrogenous substances, are entirely lost in the examination, as they quickly dissolve. The secured gluten and the settled starch are weighed together; thus the quantities are ascertained. For the determination of gluten, MM. Bolin and Robins, of Paris, have invented an ingenious instrument called an aleurometer, by which a baking process is gone through and the quantity found with ease. The ashes are determined by burning a certain quantity, which is afterwards weighed, and may reach from 1·5 to 2·2 per cent; if more than this, adulteration by mineral substances is to be suspected, and must be traced by chemical analysis.

But there are also practical tests which are of equal importance to the miller and baker, especially chemicals for improving the general appearance.

Experienced men are, of course, the most accurate judges of the feel, colour, and general appearance of good flours, but it not infrequently happens that even they are compelled to use a microscope. The principal defect in flour, and one difficult of detection, is that which causes the flowing of the dough when it does not rise, but instead, spreads itself on the sides. This may be attributed to the presence of wild garlic, the quality of the land on which the wheat grew, etc. Herr Oser, of Krems, in "Niederœsterrich," suggests an original expedient to test the quality of flour, *viz.*:—Take 16 grammes of flour from every exhibitor, and knead these singly in eight grammes of water. The best flour will give the stiffest dough.

So far as baking-flour is concerned, it should not be too fine, for fine flour bakes harder than coarse flour, being much less vaporous. Good flour should be of a yellowish colour, and much practical experience is needed for proper discrimination between the superior and inferior grades.

To test flour in order to ascertain the admixture of rye flour, potato flour, etc., the Pekar flour-tester is the most reliable. It is patented, and can only be used in the mill on payment of a yearly royalty of 1 kroner per 109 kilogrammes. Microscopical examinations also show adulterations, and for this test a magnifying power of 300 to 400 diameters is necessary. The particles of rye flour are larger than those of wheat or barley flour, but the difference in size is not very great. This examination is, therefore, not reliable, more especially as by it quality merely, not quantity, can be ascertained. It is much more easy to detect the addition of oats, millet, rice, or maize, as the starch particles of these are much more apparent, the maize starch being largest of all, and therefore most easily observed. The outer husk of millet flour is ground largely along with it. Rice flour is entirely free from husks or shells, because these shell with the gluten husk, and therefore the quantity of gluten is very small; the starch kernels are angular, and the colour of the flour is a beautiful white. Oat flour contains bran, which cannot altogether be removed. In many places oats are not ground to flour.

Wheat flour is adulterated by being mixed with rye, barley, or rice flour—especially with the latter.

Flour adulterated with bean or pea flour is known by the elliptical shape of the starch particles of the latter. Adulteration by mineral matter is immediately detected by the microscope, presenting as it does the appearance of a grey, formless mass. From practical experience I have found that reliable brands of Hungarian flour are " E.O.P.," " Concordia," and " P.W.M."

SPICED FLOUR.

Of late years our workshops have been pretty well inundated with what millers term " spiced flour." This does not seem to be confined to any one district, as I have had the misfortune to work it in Carlisle and in Scarborough. It must be a source of great loss to both miller and baker, and I have known more than one business seriously affected by the occasional use of it. From inquiry made, I find it is caused by a parasite, peculiar to California, that grows in the germs of wheat, but cannot be discovered by the naked eye. The flour milled from this particular wheat has, when baked, a peculiar spicy taste and flavour which is anything but agreeable.*

ON YEASTS AND BARMS.

As I consider flour the primary substance in the manipulation of bread, so I think it will not be out of order to place yeast next, as playing a good secondary part. The many varieties of yeasts now before the public, whether used privately or advertised by wholesale merchants, are legion. Were we to believe all the references given for, and the results said to be obtained by, the various so-called yeasts, we should be tempted to think that at last the baking community had reached that El Dorado which they have so long striven to attain. But if we are induced to try one of these fancy-named brands, we invariably find it to be but an old one newly named, and sent forth again to make more full an already well-stocked market,

---

* Since writing the above I have had a further consignment of the above-named spiced flour, which seems to be getting more prevalent than heretofore, and unless means are used to exterminate the parasite it will soon become a calamity to both millers and bakers. Being very much interested to get at the real cause of spiced flour, I have extended my inquiries regarding it. My first information was from a farmer, who says he has had over fifty years' experience in growing wheat, and he states that spiced flour is caused by hariff (or catsweed) being ground with the wheat. My other informant is a miller, who says that the complaint is caused by darnel (commonly called the weed cockle) getting amongst the wheat; the weed is quite common in certain districts of Britain. This shows the diversity of opinion that exists respecting this peculiar taste in flour, but I am still inclined to think that the parasite in the Californian wheat (as far as my practical experience is concerned) is the most probable cause.

with an "F.I.C." attached to it, to "raise" it in the estimation of the public.

That there are good and inferior brands every practical baker will admit who has had anything to do with the working of compressed yeasts; but I believe that the good brands outweigh the inferior ones. I could mention half-a-dozen brands that have all the qualities a modern baker could desire; and in the following chapter I will try and show the reader what a really good yeast should be, in as plain language as the subject I am treating of will allow. And as this work is written for the special use of journeymen bakers, I am vain enough to hope that it may assist in the removal of some of the stumbling-blocks that beset their way, and may prove a benefit to a few of my brothers in trade.

PARISIAN BARM.

Let us take our first lesson on Parisian barm.

The baker should see that his barm tub is clean and dry before it is used. Put one gallon of water, heated to about 140° F., into a pan or earthen pot; weigh two pounds of crushed malt, and place it in the water. Cover the mixture up and let the malt steep for about three hours. One hour before you intend to make your barm—*i.e.*, after the malt has been steeping two hours—put a large pan containing three gallons of water upon the fire. When this boils add two ounces of good, fresh hops; this must be boiled for twenty minutes. While the hop water is boiling, strain the malt water into the barm tub through a hair sieve, squeezing each lot of malt in your hands so thoroughly as to leave no water or juice in it. (The sieve should be placed over the tub, resting on sticks lying across its top). After this add to the malt water as much flour as can be stirred in it, using the barm stick to stir with. Next put the boiling hop water through a sieve over the malt and flour water, and stir well. The baker must be very expeditious in scalding his malt water and flour, as one of the necessary points in the manufacture of this barm is to ensure its being thoroughly scalded. Assistance is required in the removal of the pot or pan from the fire, and in putting the liquid into the tub, while the operator stands with the barm stick ready in his hand, and commences to stir the ingredients as soon as may be, so that the flour be thoroughly scalded. Too strong a flour scalds badly; therefore the baker should note what flour answers best, and stick to it.

Instead of putting the hops direct into the water, many bakers place them inside a small linen bag made for the purpose. In this way they require half-an-hour to boil; the bag should be pressed and squeezed against the pan sides before it is taken out. The operator then throws the boiling hop water upon the malt water and flour, and stirs as before.

Supposing the time to be five o'clock in the afternoon, the tub, covered with a sack or two to prevent the mass from growing too cold, is put aside till next morning, when it should be stirred with the hand, the thick or jellied parts that adhere to the sides being all thoroughly mixed. See that the liquid (it cannot yet be termed barm) is not too hot for setting away; the right heat is about 85°. Add half a gallon of barm, previously made, and stir well; then put the liquid aside in a nice temperature to work itself ready. This should take not more than eight or ten hours, though much depends on the heat of the surrounding atmosphere. When about ready you will see a thin froth start generally at one side of the tub and gradually work over to the other side, though I have seen it start to spread from the middle. By following this method, circumstances being favourable, you cannot fail to have good Parisian barm.

SOUR PARISIAN BARM.

Barm of this nature has a dull, worked-out, greasy appearance, with little or no life in it. Where the trade is small, and will only allow of the barm being made twice a week, I should advise the baker to procure three or four earthen pots, and when the barm is ready, divide what is required for each day into these pots, along with the store of barm required to start the next making. In doing this he will, in great measure, protect himself against harbouring impure ferments. But Parisian barm should, if possible, be made every day.

ON "BRINGING AWAY" PARISIAN BARM WITHOUT ANY PREVIOUSLY-MADE BARM BEING MIXED WITH THE FRESHLY-MADE LIQUID.

This can with skilful hands be easily done, but I should not advise the amateur to adopt this method until he has thoroughly mastered the difficulties presented by fermentation. In places where it is done — and there are such places — a recess, sufficiently large to hold a small pot of the size of about a half-gallon tin, is built in the front of the oven. Proceed as follows:—

After your liquid has been scalded and made, take three pints of it and place it in the above-mentioned recess. Keep it at a fixed temperature, and stir it up three or four times a day. After the first day add four ounces of moist cane sugar, and continue stirring occasionally till you see it beginning to ferment. Then let it ferment till ready; it should again be stirred and kept in a warm atmosphere till the fermenting process is completed.

As I said before, a skilful Parisian barm-maker can do it, but it should not be attempted by an amateur, as both knowledge and skill are required to bring it away.

VIRGIN BARM.

Virgin barm, or bastard barm, as it is sometimes called, is made in somewhat the same way as Parisian barm, with the exception that there is neither malt nor hops used. It is nothing more than scalded flour; but I have seen barm of this kind make splendid bread. It should be made frequently, as it is apt to weaken if not kept up with a good store of Parisian barm—*i.e.*, the three quarts of barm given to it to cause fermentation or to make it work. The mode of manufacture is entirely the same as that required in making Parisian barm, and it has this in its favour—it is easily made, and is cheap.

Boil three gallons of water in a pan, and sift what flour you think will be required, and put it in a tub; pour the boiling water upon it, during which it should be well stirred, and will, if properly scalded, grow thick during the process. Some bakers only take two gallons for the first scald, taking the remaining gallon for a second scalding. The scalding must be thorough, or it is useless. When the heat is down to about 86°, start it with three quarts of previously-made barm. This is really a capital barm, but, like others, requires attention.

MALT AND HOP BARM,

or composition barm, as it is in some places called, is another good barm; there is no mystery or difficulty in connection with its manufacture.

Procure a large pan, and put into it three gallons of water. Sift through a fine sieve two pounds of crushed malt, and put what remains in the sieve into the water in the pan, along with two ounces of good fresh hops. Either boil this for an hour, or put it into the oven the last thing at night, and remove it the first thing next morning. Strain it through a fine, sieve when cold enough for use, squeezing it well with the hand till no moisture remains in the malt and hops. Set the liquid apart till it is thoroughly cold; the temperature may be 68° or 70° F. The sifted malt, together with a pint of previously-made malt and hop barm, is now to be mixed with the liquid to start it to work (or set away).

This barm must be cool when worked, and in working it should come up with a nice frothy cauliflower head. I have made this barm set away with an ounce of German yeast with good results; but the other is preferable.

This barm is best adapted for potato fermentation. I have tested it, in setting a ferment—quite cold—two days before using it, with only a pint and a half of barm to eighteen stone of flour, and it produced a loaf that was, in flavour, colour and texture, all that a practical man could desire.

STORE.

Store is a flour barm that was, some twenty-four years ago, in general use in Scotland (at least in the south); but now, unless by some of the very old school, it is seldom used, Parisian and virgin barm being easier to make and having better keeping qualities. Still, when this barm was all right, I have seen very good bread made from it, but I never liked its flavour. It was mostly used for potato ferments. I have seen tub after tub of it thrown away, especially when there was an atmospheric change.

Boil three gallons of water, into which (in a bag made for the purpose) put four ounces of good hops. After half-an-hour's boiling, squeeze the bag against the sides of the pan, to get rid of all juice from the hops. The store-stick should be in the tub with the quantity of flour required, which quantity a baker can only know by experience; then take one half of the boiling water from the fire, and give the mixture the first scalding. Stir till you can stir no longer, which will soon be, as the store has to be as thick as ordinary batch dough; when the first scald is completed, hand your store-stick to an assistant and let him have a try. The remainder of the boiling hop water may now be taken; see that a proper scald is effected, for on this the quality of the store depends. The store should now be about the size of pie dough; when properly scalded, put it away, as for other barms, covered with a sack, till nearly cold; then add half a gallon of previously prepared store, to set away. Or, by keeping the batter at a regular heat, this barm can be brought away by itself; also by stirring it up in the tub till fermentation ensues. Then let it work itself ready, when it should rise in the tub about two inches, and drop the same distance.

This is a most difficult barm to make, as it requires a very skilful man, and will soon go sour if the tubs are not properly scalded and cleansed. I have seen a tub of this store spoiled by a single accidental knock during the early stages of fermentation.

AMERICAN PATENT YEAST.

Take half a pound of hops and two pailfuls of water; mix and boil till the liquid is reduced one half; strain the decoction into a tub, and when lukewarm add half a peck of malt. In the meantime put the drained-off hops again into two pailfuls of water and boil as before, till the liquid is reduced one half; then strain the hot liquid into a tub. (The heat will not injuriously affect malt previously mixed with tepid water.) When the liquid has cooled to about 85° F., strain off the malt and add to the liquid two quarts of patent yeast of a previous making. This should make five gallons of good yeast, which will be ready for use the day after it is made. It takes about eight hours to make, and gives very little trouble to the baker.

BREWERS' BARM

has fallen greatly into disuse, and Parisian barm, patent barm, virgin barm and compressed yeast have taken the lead. Brewers' barm requires to be worked with a potato ferment, and potato ferments I consider to be things of the past. They have answered their purpose, I dare say, very well; but this is another instance of the "survival of the fittest." Potato ferments must give way to better and more modern methods. These ferments are mostly used in Scotland and in some parts of London. It is, indeed, strange that two of our largest bread-producing centres should be the last to give up the old, mediæval style of doing things. Old customs die hard; still, I have seen potato ferments of service when used in weak or soft flour. But flour ferments, quarter sponges, half sponges, and full sponges are the order of the day. I never took very kindly to brewers' barm, as I fancied it left a peculiar taste in the bread. In Liverpool and its vicinity, brewers' barm is in common use, and it has this peculiarity, that a certain amount of salt is used with the ferment while it is working.

GERMAN YEAST.

German yeasts—their name is legion—have entirely revolutionised the baking trade—at any rate, on this side of the border. Our trade is in this respect in no way different from others. New appliances, ingenious instruments, and complicated machinery, in connection with trades and handicrafts, have constantly arisen, and are continuing to increase, some undoubtedly being great improvements and supplying urgent needs, others being of a less beneficial character. But be that as it may, the introduction of German yeast has been a great and acknowledged boon to the baking trade.

The name German yeast includes, to a baker's mind, all kinds of compressed yeast, English, Scotch, French or German. ood brands come from Germany, yeast that the manufacturers may well be proud of. But there are an equal number of inferior brands, which are generally used for retail purposes, and sold to housewives and people out of the trade. When they get inferior brands of yeast to work, the flour is usually blamed; they do not take into consideration their own incapacity, or the quality of the yeast they are using.

SCOTCH YEAST

is made in some of the breweries in the north of Scotland. Some twelve years ago I used this kind of yeast, but at that time did not like it—it was too weak and feeble, having very small powers of fermentation about it. The Scotch manufacturers have, however, very much improved their methods of making yeast since then, and are now producing an article which is taking a high stand in the market.

FRENCH YEAST.

Some really good brands of yeast come from France. But it would be unfair to specify any; France keeps well abreast with every other country in manufacturing this particular article.

ENGLISH COMPRESSED YEAST.

There is a particular brand of compressed yeast manufactured in England that will more than hold its own for quality and price with any of those above referred to. I have used it daily for twelve months, and can testify to its merits. It has good strength and flavour, and is good in every way—more especially when the reasonableness of its price is taken into consideration.*

COMPRESSED YEASTS WHEN STALE AND UNFIT FOR USE.

Now that the greater part of the bread made in the United Kingdom is fermented with compressed yeasts, a short dissertation on the appearance of yeast when seen in the above-named undesirable condition will, I think, be of use to the practical baker. Continental yeasts, when seen in this state, are, as a rule, dark, soft, and clammy; the odour becomes loathsome and disagreeable, and there is none of that pleasant, fresh, barmy smell, so much admired by those bakers who use it. The softening of yeasts of this class, and their bad appearance, are said to be due to incipient germination, caused by excessive heat and moisture. I may likewise add that the same disagreeable results may be brought about by rough usage, such as carelessly throwing the yeast about, etc., which causes it to germinate and feed upon its own substance, thereby weakening its properties and in a very short time rendering it unfit for any practical use.

Compressed yeasts made in Britain, when bad or stale, present quite a different appearance. I may say that I have studied the appearance and practical results of these in their various stages of decomposition for a number of years, and have found that the British-made yeasts, when in this state, become very dry; the temperature of the yeast is also high, and it is

---

* The increased daily demand for the best brands of English compressed yeast conclusively proves my assertion. I would invite all who use foreign yeasts to compare the above yeasts with the best French, German and Danish productions, and I have no doubt as to the result. Why send money out of the country when an article of superior quality, and at a cheaper price, can be bought at your doors? Besides, you have the satisfaction of knowing that you are helping to encourage home industries.

warm to the touch. The colour becomes white, and, when the weakening process goes on apace, instead of softening like continental yeasts when passing from the healthy to the unhealthy stages, it becomes dry and crumbly, and entirely unfit for use.

If compressed yeast is kept in the vicinity of salt, the action of the atmosphere on this commodity will render the yeast soft, and in a short time it will become useless. To prove this, place a small piece of fresh yeast amongst a little salt, when it will soon begin to liquefy. Care must therefore be taken, and arrangement made to keep yeast in as pure an atmosphere as the conditions of the bakery will permit.

My motive in writing this short article on the appearance of bad yeasts in their various stages of deterioration, is to put the baker on his guard, and to warn him against using them in too debilitated a condition. Recently I saw it stated in one of our trade journals that a practical man has no guide to aid him in this dilemma, save his judgment and experience of smell and taste; likewise, that there are no rough-and-ready tests that have any degree of reliability. Well, if this be true, our modern practical bread baker is in a very precarious, unenviable position. No better, simpler, or surer test could a workman desire, surely, than that given in a former work of mine, "The Bread and Biscuit Baker," on page 11. So far as my own experience goes, and that of those who have wisely adopted the test, I have never known it to fail.

For the benefit of those who have not read that work, I here repeat the description of the test :—

"Procure a clean cup or tumbler; half fill it with warm water, temperature 100°; place an ounce of lump sugar in the water, and, when this has dissolved, add one ounce of the suspected yeast. The yeast will first sink to the 'bottom; if in a workable state it will rise to the top in two minutes. If a much longer time is required for rising, dependence should not be placed upon its fermenting qualities. The strength of the yeast you are testing is shown entirely by the time it takes to rise to the top of the water."

HOW TO KEEP YEAST PURE.

In the year 1680, yeast was found to contain organic matter; but scientists did not give it attention till M. Pasteur undertook the study of it. It is from him that we have obtained our chief knowledge of ferments, and one of the most useful discoveries of scientific chemistry is the knowledge how to keep yeast pure.

Where there is difficulty in keeping yeast pure, one of M. Pasteur's suggestions may perhaps be valuable: it is especially applicable during warm weather. The yeast, he suggests, should be grown in sweetened water, in successive growths, a small percentage of tartaric acid being added; also by growing it in wort, adding a few drops of phonel. It requires care and attention, and is a very valuable method in warm climates and weathers.

LEAVEN

is nothing more nor less than flour and water, stirred together and kept in a warm place until fermentation commences. Every time the baker makes bread, a certain quantity should be kept back in an earthen pot for the next sponge.

The use of leaven is supposed to have originated in Egypt. It is very seldom used in this country now, although in some parts of Cumberland it occurs in the manufacture of a particular kind of brown bread. In some European countries where yeast is not easily obtained leaven is used. Sailors use it on long voyages. But, like most things where fermentation is concerned, care and cleanliness must be observed. But let leaven be ever so well manufactured, the bread made from it has always a rank, sour taste, and is not to be compared with yeast-made bread.

The degrees of heat given in the preceding pages for starting barms to work, etc., are for use in winter. Less heat will suffice in summer. The temperature of the bakehouse will likewise have to be taken into consideration. This also applies to sponging.

SALT.

Salt, or chloride of sodium, has more to do in checking fermentation and seasoning bread than most practical bakers will admit.

I have no doubt that when the practical baker studies chemistry, as in time the exigencies of his trade must force him to do, and he thoroughly understands the properties and constituent parts of this necessary—but nearly altogether neglected—substance, it will take a higher place in the estimation of practical men that it at present occupies. In fact, when conversing with men on the respective qualities of bread, salt is rarely mentioned.

Flour and yeast are, I confess, the main factors in bread making; but I really think that salt plays third part in producing the "staff of life."

Salt is obtained in various ways—as fossil or rock salt; from the boiling or evaporation of salt springs; and from the sea. In a pure state it consists of 60 per cent. of chlorine, and 40 per cent. of sodium. Salt, with food, acts as a tonic, aids the digestive powers of the stomach, and assists in assimilating fatty substances. It is, therefore, an important article.

WATER

being a necessary element in bread manufacture, a few words must be said about it. I have noticed that bread made under the same conditions, and with the same brands of flour and yeast, varies so much in different districts, that I have been inclined to doubt the similarity of the ingredients. The only reason that I can assign for this difference of quality is that the chemical properties of the water employed are different; and a baker's practical experience will very soon tide him over this difficulty. Water taken from a boiler that is built on a chaffer or furnace should not be used for sponging, as it is liable to get too much boiled, by which it loses part of its chemical properties. Anyone can easily prove this by making tea with water that has boiled for half an hour or longer, and then with water that has just come to the boil. The flavour of the tea made from the latter will be far superior to that made from the former; and what applies to tea, correspondingly applies to bread.

Now, having introduced to the reader the various qualities of flour, yeast, salt, and water, let me blend them together as a whole in the endeavour to produce bread that will satisfy alike the palate of a pampered epicure, and the trained, scrutinising eye of a practical baker.

FERMENTATION.*

The meaning of the word "fermentation" should be of great interest to the modern journeyman baker. But if the simple question as to its true meaning is put, out of every hundred answers how many will be correct?

Pasteur, the renowned chemist and physiologist, says:—
"My most decided opinion on the nature of alcoholic fermentation is: The chemical act of fermentation is essentially a correlative phenomenon of a vital act beginning and ending with it. I think there is never any alcoholic fermentation without there being at the same time organisation, development, multiplication of globules, or the continued consecutive life of globules already formed."

The process has for its object either the manufacture of bread, or of an alcoholic product in a more or less concentrated form—both very similar in action during the earlier stages. It communicates with the growth and multiplication of the fermenting germs contained in the minute organisms floating in the air, and the inorganic constituents of the water; and all the changes are produced by heat.

Dr. Ducleaux, of Paris, in his "Handbook on Fermentation," says that:

"The history of microbes can be reduced to an examination of the nutritive requirements, and of their means of satisfying them. It is there that the great difference between them and the higher animals is to be found. The latter are also formed of cells, individually nearly as small as those of ferments; but these cells, which possess various properties, and are bound up in various tissues, are naturally subjected, through the medium of the blood, the nerves, and the muscles, to a series of profound

* See also Appendix.

and complex actions, on which physiology will gradually throw light. The study of microbes is exempt from such complications. Here the cells are free and independent; their principal —I might say their only—occupation is that of feeding. The latter only depends on questions of alimentary matter, of temperature, of moisture, which we can easily master. The problem is, therefore, relatively speaking, an easy one. Let us study it carefully. We shall be rewarded by the discovery that its solution, once found, can be applied in a general manner, and will supply a key to the understanding of the nutrition of the higher animals.

"This nutrition necessitates the presence of a certain number of different elements, which may be divided under four heads. Every cell contains nitrogenous organic matter, non-nitrogenous, and mineral matter, thus requiring for nutrition (1) nitrogen, (2) carbo-hydrates, (3) minerals. Moreover, every cell breathes, thus needing (4) gaseous aliments.

"I will begin with the last, and show what a fertile field of study it and the others open out.

"At first it may be thought that yeast does not breathe, in the sense that we usually attach to the word, that is to say, that it does not require oxygen.

"In order that a fresh fermentation may be produced, it has been shown that the brewer takes the seed from a former fermentation, where the liquid is saturated with carbonic acid and does not contain air. When once it is in the wort the yeast almost immediately produces carbonic acid, and is in an atmosphere where there is no oxygen. This has been taking place for centuries, and the yeast at present in use seems to have descended from that which the brewers in Egypt used 6,000 years ago, by a series of successive generations, and a process which must apparently have taken place in the absence of oxygen."

Dr. Ducleaux continues to say that:

"If a beetroot be put in carbonic acid, it will produce alcohol; cherries, plums, apples, any sweet fruit or sacchariferous plants treated similarly will still have the sugar they contain partly turned into alcohol and carbonic acid under these new conditions of life.

"The only difference between these and yeast is that they are much less able to exist in the absence of air, that they do not carry fermentation so far, and that they stop or die before having transformed all their sugar. But these are merely differences in degree; the main point is to recognise that the relation between alcoholic fermentation and the exclusion of air is common to a long series of living organisms.

"Yeast is one of the terms of this series, but not the last; for we have seen that after all it requires a little air, and I shall point out microbes, to which air is not only useless, but injurious.

"Fermentation has ceased, I hope, to be for us an isolated and mysterious process, incapable of explanation or interpretation. It is the consequence of nutrition and of the existence of the cells under special conditions, which differ in most cases from those of their ordinary life, and to which yeast appears to easily adapt itself during the course of its fermenting career. But, as we have seen, yeast by its life in contact with air approaches nearly to the nature of ordinary plants; also that plants existing in carbonic acid possess the properties of yeast. Thus a continuous chain connects all these cells so dissimilar in appearance, their only difference being the fact that they present in greater or less degrees the two fundamental aspects of life with air, and life without air."

In the "Zeitschrift für das Gesammte Brauwesen" for 1888 there appeared a critical examination of the difference between

Pasteur's and Hansen's views on the yeast question by Jörgensen —who is himself a high authority on this important subject—in which he gives great prominence to Hansen's views on fermentation. Ferdinand Hueppe, in a lengthy article replying to the above, claims to have put forth the same theory simultaneously with Hansen. Hueppe says :—

"The prominence thus given to Hansen's claims in a German journal startled me, as nowhere have Hansen's deserts been more unreservedly acknowledged than among ourselves. But why the opportunity should have been taken for a side-hit at Koch and his pupils, I confess myself at a loss to understand. And I feel in duty bound to set the matter right, whilst making all due acknowledgment of the progress in the physiology and technology of fermentation for which we are indebted to Hansen. Amongst Koch's pupils I formerly stood alone in my devotion to problems of fermentative physiology. But my researches in milk decompositions were dependent on Koch only so far as regards the method; and on my later works Koch exerted no influence whatever. The charge of taking 'the same indefinite view' as Pasteur, therefore, points in a special manner to myself. Pasteur, in the study of lactic fermentation, which commenced in his famous 'Study of Fermentation,' endeavoured to show that every specific type of fermentation is the work of a special 'ferment;' and next that in this sense there is an alcoholic, a lactic, and a butyric fermentation. Subsequently he left this point somewhat obscure, and brought anaërobism more to the front. 'All fermentation is dependent on exclusion of air' was an oft-repeated watchword of the new French school of pathology. But, to improve on Pasteur, the nature of the ferment-organisms, in regard alike of their chemico-physiological conditions and their specific properties, must be kept in view. As regards the latter, the credit of having taken the first steps in advance unquestionably belongs to Brefeld. He was the first to follow, uninterruptedly from the germ, the morphology of organisms occurring in fermentations, and to show that fermentation and the resulting chemical changes were the work of *quasi*-specific micro-organisms, while as yet Pasteur had treated the subject very superficially. Among budding-fungi the existence of surface and bottom yeasts led Pasteur to admit specific differences in yeasts, of which he recognised eight species. He thought also that more would be discovered, but he was rather vague on the subject—he supposed that all the cells in a yeast culture had certain properties in common, and also that every cell had its own distinctive characteristics ('des caractères propres qui la distinguent'), which by successive cultures might be made to originate new types. Thus in the same breath Pasteur talks of specific peculiarities and the variability of species of saccharomyces. All honour is due to Pasteur for having shown by his experiments in technical practice that industrial yeasts are rendered impure by bacteria, and that such bacterial organisms, some of which he described, may cause diseases in beers and wines. But this was not going far enough, and it was reserved for Hansen to show that wild yeasts are each derived from a single germ or spore. Hansen thus determined that wild and cultivated yeasts exhibit specific characteristics, and that different kinds of alcoholic fermentation depend on specifically distinct forms of saccharomyces. After several years of preliminary research Hansen published the first definite exposition of his labours in 1883 on bacteria. Cohn first addressed himself to supply the morphological omissions of Pasteur, and believed himself to have discovered—what, in part, was discovered quite independently by Lister—that bacterial decompositions are the work of eight different kinds of bacterial organisms. In this sense we learned to recognise an agent of lactic fermentation, another of butyric fermentation, and so forth. The unsatisfactory character of the method employed, and the view propounded in the meantime by Nageli, of the indefinite capacity differentiation of ferment organisms, led to my own investigations of the changes in milk. These were ready for the press at the end of March, 1888, and I never set eyes upon them again until the appearance of Part II. of 'Mittheilungen aus Kaiserliche Gesundheit-amte,' my prolonged absence from Germany debarring me from making any corrections therein. The work, however, was quite coeval with Hansen's. In it I showed by exact demonstration that definite types of decomposition are the work of definite *quasi*-specific micro-organisms, and that differences in such decompositions are due to specific biological differences in the organisms inducing them. In respect of budding-fungi and bacteria, this more correct view was propounded by Hansen and myself at one and the same time, and quite independently of one another. And this fact alone is, I think, sufficient to show the impossibility of any serious incompatibility in our opinions."

The above extracts show that dissimilar views are still held by scientists of the new school of fermentative physiology, and the reader will see what reliance can as yet be placed upon the opinions of scientists engaged in this mysterious but all-absorbing theme of speculative theory—fermentation.

SPONGING.

Sponging is a blending together of flour, yeast and water, with the addition of salt, mixed into one substance, and practically carried through the successive stages *at the proper degree of heat.* No amount of theory will compass this, unless the operator has the practical part of his business well in hand.

SUNDAY SPONGING.

Sunday night sponging is one of the baker's grievances, and is gradually drawing itself to the front and forcing itself both upon the trade and the public. That it is a hardship for bakers no one can gainsay.

Some twenty years ago a body of philanthropic gentlemen took up this matter, but their ideas were vague and proved to be illusory, as the system they advocated was based upon the old style of long and all-night-and-day sponging. The sudden atmospheric changes our country is subject to (and practical bakers who have charge of the sponging department know what care is required to guard against such changes) was one of the leading forces which helped to quash this much-needed reform. The mode adopted was as follows:—

To work up one sack of flour, the quantity of water required for a sponge, Scotch style, was heated to a certain degree, which would be, of course, pretty cool, but not sufficiently cold to starve the sponge. One quart of Parisian barm was added, with three pounds of salt; and the sponge was made pretty stiff. On the Sunday the foreman came and looked at the sponge, and if he thought it was working too quickly, or too slowly, he would regulate it accordingly, either taking sacks off, or putting sacks upon the trough; and there was always plenty of hot water that could be put under the trough if required. But if there was no change in the weather these things were seldom required.

This I know is too old-fashioned a plan for a modern bakery, and would not now be accepted by the trade.

My suggestion would be to abolish Sunday work altogether, adopt compressed yeast for Monday's work, and let one or two men (according to the size of the firm) come to the bakehouse about two hours before the usual time, and set a flying or quick sponge. (See page 36). It can be got ready in an hour and a half, and I am sure that bread worked in this way would, under a practical foreman, give satisfaction. Some, I know, are averse to German yeast, but there are plenty of so-called German yeasts of good quality made in England, that will answer quite as well. In my opinion it gives a nicer flavour; but those who are averse to working it (and I know of a good many in Scotland) should use Parisian barm. One or two men could be told off to do duty on Sunday, and they could get as many quarters as were required with Parisian barm, to be ready at an earlier hour on Monday morning. Then one or two should come early on Monday and set what sponges were required for the first round of bread. This arrangement would allow at least a few men to have Sundays for themselves; every little helps, and if any of these practices or modes, or any other arrangement of a feasible nature were once started, I am sure we have men in the trade skilful enough to bring this kind of sponging to a successful issue.

The recent movement in the baking trade, notably in England, Ireland, Scotland, and America, for lessening the number of hours a baker has to work, and for the alleviation of other grievances connected with the trade, is a sure sign that the baker is at last taking the initiative; success in the attempt to gain a higher position, and take a stand as a body of practical workmen, is merely a matter of time. Let us hope, then, that the day is not far distant when bakers will enjoy the rest of the Sabbath day, like any other tradesmen or civilised Christians. And let us work, as well as hope, for that end.

ON INCREASING AND DECREASING SPONGES.

It frequently happens that after the afternoon sponges have been set, a material change takes place in the bread orders for the following day. Either an extra order has been booked, or the vans have not been so successful in their day's sales as the vanmen anticipated; or the shop trade may fluctuate; or other things may happen that produce an accumulation of surplus bread. Take the first case, where an increase of the sponge already set is required. Suppose the extra bread required is twenty 4lb. loaves. Now each pail of water when worked with the requisite amount of flour produces, on an average, twenty 4lb. loaves. The salt required to season one pail of water (at the recognised rate of 3lbs. to the sack) would be a little under 10 ounces. When doughing add this extra pail of water and salt to the usual quantity of water required to take the sponge—all the water to be at an advanced temperature of eight degrees over the usual heat required. Then after the dough is made let it lie an extra half-hour before weighing off. This will give your required increase of twenty loaves. But the operator must not expect the bread made after this manner to have the same bold appearance as if the barm for this particular batch had not had the extra amount of salt and water to carry. The appearance of the dough, technically speaking, will have a greasy look, and it will be inclined to slide. On the other hand, suppose less bread is required and the sponge has to be taken down: allow the same proportion as for the increase, *viz.*, twenty 4lb. loaves. Now, suppose it requires three pails of water at night and two pails in the morning with 3lbs. of salt to take up 20 stone of flour, one pail of water, with the corresponding amount of salt, must be kept from the sponge; the temperature to be eight degrees colder than the operator would take the sponge if the full complement of water was given; this will give the required result of twenty loaves less, and so on in proportion. I do not advocate this particular system, except in cases of emergency such as I have suggested at the beginning of this paragraph, and it particularly applies to the usual style of working in Scotland, where Parisian barm is the motive power used in fermenting sponges. In warm weather, when less salt and water is used than the amount of barm given is expected to ferment, great care and judgment is required or sour bread is likely to result. In England, where compressed yeast is the order of the day, the case is different, as any increase of orders can easily be met, and in a short time, by applying extra yeast to a quick or flying sponge. But any deviation from the required style or system recognised by the trade (providing that system is sound and practically based, and in harmony with the law of cause and effect) must have its bad effect on the flavour and general appearance of the bread.

SOURNESS IN BREAD.

Of all the evils the baking trade has to contend with, sourness in bread is, I think, the worst. Some of my readers will very likely have heard the story of the two master bakers in Scotland.

One day Tammas Smith was walking down the high street of a Scottish town, when he saw a brother in trade, Geordie Robinson, pacing up and down in front of his own shop, evidently in anything but an agreeable frame of mind. When Tammas got up to Geordie, he said :—

"Weel, Geordie, hoo's a' wi' 'ye this mornin' ? What makes ye luik sae agitated, mun ? "

"Agitated!" exclaimed Geordie. "Oor batch's oot, an' the breed's soor, an' I canna stand the smell o't i' my ain shop!"

No wonder that Geordie was agitated, for of all the smells that annoy a baker a "soor" smell is the most aggravating. Certainly it is not Otto of Roses, Eau de Cologne, or Jockey Club. If anyone wishes to beg a favour from a baker, let him be sure to learn that his bread is sweet.

The causes of sourness in bread are so numerous that it is difficult to fix upon one specially. But its origin can be traced to germs of specific ferments, such as butyric and lactic ferments, which produce a certain amount of acidity; but the two causes which I consider most common are carelessness and want of cleanliness. If a bakehouse is not kept clean, and is not regularly whitewashed, the atmosphere becomes contaminated with germs, which enter into sponges, dough, barms, etc.; in fact, there is no telling where they may alight and propagate. They are as contagious as a fever, and it is as difficult a thing to expel them from a bakehouse as it is easy for them to enter one.

I remember, some years ago, in a small town named Maxwelltown, adjoining Dumfries, there was a rather large firm turning over between 60 and 70 sacks a week; and I well recollect what consternation arose when it was hinted that this firm's bread was sour, and had been so for a week. I did not believe the report at first, as the firm was noted for good, sweet, well-flavoured bread, and there were two good skilful men at the head of the bakery, though they were, for all I know, ignorant of chemistry. On inquiry the report proved to be too true; and they tried everything they knew to stop the ravages of these germs of specific ferments, such as fresh barm, fresh stores of barm, scalding out troughs and the barm tubs, hot lime, etc.—in fact, everything but the right thing. The sourness continued day after day for six weeks, till at last I believe they fumigated the bakehouse, whitewashed the walls, and used excessive cleanliness; then, and not till then, they exterminated these enemies of the baker.

Another cause of sourness in bread is too much warmth in setting the sponge, and allowing it to lie too long before it is taken. Still another lies in adding too warm water when taking up your sponge. Experience and a thermometer will obviate both these difficulties. Again, I have seen a sponge taken up in a healthy, ripe condition, and, some old scrap from a previous batch having been allowed to be mixed with it, it has turned out in anything but a satisfactory state. Another cause is impure or weak yeast or barm, most particularly so in flour and Parisian barm. But a good preventive of weakness in Parisian barm is to make it every day, if the amount required will allow you to do so.

Weak or bad flour is still another cause for sourness in bread. I have used flour so weak that I have not dared to let the sponge even turn, while with other flour it has had to be twice dropped before being taken. It may fitly be mentioned here that there is no hard and fast rule for a baker to go by, to know exactly when a sponge is ready, for all depends on the quality of the flour and the yeast employed. I find that sour milk is a great enemy to healthy dough, and when it is allowed to get mixed in barm or sponges, the impure germs are speedily propagated, and sour bread results. Causes for this disease in bread can be enumerated, but quite sufficient has been said to put the baker on his guard. Two things to be avoided let me again impress upon the baker—carelessness and uncleanliness.

The appearance of sour bread is the reverse of inviting. In some cases where it is sour it clings or dries on the sides of the loaves before it can be baked, and has a dull, glazed appearance.

Sometimes bread springs out of shape, and is liable to take no colour on the top, presenting an altogether boiled appearance, and turning out in a very untradesmanlike manner, with decided lack of finish.

Bread should always be thoroughly baked, though not baked too much. Underbaked bread has a tendency to sourness when it is kept, for the underbaked part in the centre of the loaf will be " claggy " and is liable to ferment, and be quite unpalatable.

UNRIPE SPONGES

will next be treated upon—jimp, or still-born sponges, as I have sometimes heard them called.

Unripe sponges are the exact opposites of overworked sponges. A modern baker, however, seldom allows himself to be annoyed by their manufacture, as the spirit of competition is too keen to admit of the return to the old times of waiting and cooking unripe sponges. Still, cases occur when he cannot help himself, and he has a " jimp " sponge.

Waiting for a sponge is like waiting for a train, and if one has any important business to transact the delay is both tedious and annoying. But if a baker attempts to take a sponge before it is ready he may be sure of the invariable result. If the sponge is very unripe, there is, as likely as not, the necessary heating of boards, a second rolling up, happed up with sacks, the waiting, and the gripping of the dough to see if it is getting any life into it or beginning to move ; and after all the coaxing, heating and happing, the bread turns out heavy and sodden, with a dark pile and foxy appearance—in very truth, still-born. Thus a baker taking an unripe sponge is in no sense further forward than if he were content to leave it to work by itself into a healthy and properly ripe sponge. If the oven is in the usual degree of heat, the loaf's top crust is of a dirty black colour, and the bread when cut tastes claggy, as the protoplasm, or essence of life, has not been to any extent propagated in the ferments throughout the dough. Then again, an unripe sponge never gives that nice, healthy, inviting appearance one likes to note in bread, nor the nutty flavour one expects to taste in a well manipulated loaf.

Therefore, from unripe sponges and sour bread, good Lord, deliver us!

As a safeguard against both, I would advise brother tradesmen to stick to the one brand of yeast—if compressed—and flour, if both answer their purpose; for a skilful baker will soon know how to work both flour and yeast, and to extract from them, as regards strength, colour and flavour, all that is in them. Do not, if it can be avoided, shift from one brand to another, as it is in the constant change of flour and yeast that sourness has the chance of entering. Some yeasts work with a fierce, rank strength; others, again, work in a feeble, dead-slow manner. The same remarks are nearly applicable to flour. Do not, unless compelled, keep continually changing, or your chances of success are very remote.

FLOUR FERMENTS.

As we have discarded potatoes in ferments, we will proceed to give the formula for flour ferments, which are a great help to bakers, should they have the misfortune to be working soft flour. It likewise imparts a nice flavour to the bread.

To make twenty stone of flour into bread: See that your ferment tub is nice and clean. Put into it a small scoop of flour—about four pounds. Put two gallons of boiling water upon the flour in the tub; add, when the flour is thoroughly scalded, sufficient cold water to cool it down to 90° F.;

take a gallon of store or Parisian barm, and mix all together; then keep it covered with a sack in a warm place till ready. This is generally set between ten and eleven in the morning, and taken at four in the afternoon.

German yeast can be used in the flour ferment instead of Parisian barm. Ferment eight ounces to the same quantity of water and flour.

QUARTER SPONGES TO TAKE UP ONE SACK OF FLOUR.

Put one gallon of water at about 90° F. into the quarter tub with half a gallon of Parisian barm, and mix all together into a good stiff sponge. Keep in a warm place, covered with a sack, till ready. Set at one o'clock; to be taken at four. Then add sufficient water, at the required temperature, with 2lbs. of salt; thoroughly mix all together, and make a good dry sponge. When the sponge is ready, add the requisite quantity of water and salt, which should be about 6 gallons of water and from 1lb. to 1½lb. of salt.

Before proceeding to give the modern method of sponging, let me impress upon my readers the necessity for using rice flour, mixed with fine flour, for dusting and rolling up. Never use it for moulding, as it gives a dull, dark appearance to the crust of the loaf when baked; but for dusting the troughs and boards, and in rolling up—especially if the sponge be unripe, or when soft flour is employed—rice flour is invaluable. Also let me state that seventeen gallons of water are required to take up twenty stone of flour. This is the average, the amount varying with the strength of the flour. Let the baker see that the compressed yeast is not roughly handled; it is sometimes spoiled if dropped upon the ground. Too much care in handling cannot be taken. Keep it, also, in a cool place of even temperature, especially in warm weather.

When milk is required for bread, such as milk bread, diet bread, etc., buttermilk should be used; but if it cannot be procured condensed milk can be substituted, although it does not answer so well, as it does not contain sufficient acid to counteract the soda.

When condensed milk is used the bread must be baked in a sharper oven than if it had been doughed with buttermilk. The baker will be amply repaid for the greatest care and attention in these matters, for has he not the satisfaction of knowing that he has done his best (and angels can do no more), and that the bread produced must be of a superior quality to what it would have proved had he left its manufacture to chance or accident?

Let it also be remembered that more salt is required to season strong flour than for ordinary or weak flour, to produce a loaf of equal texture, on account of the extra quantity of water needed to work up such flour.

MODERN METHOD OF SPONGING.

In firms of any note the old style of sponging would not be tolerated. When it was necessary to prepare the search for the potato ferment, and cautiously pour the liquid, or ferment, into the search before squeezing the unbroken potatoes (if by chance any should be underboiled), the operator was afraid lest any potato skins should get into the sponge water, and was compelled, if by accident this happened, to hunt in the water for the offending skin with vigour and persistency, while the sponge water was cooling and time being wasted.

The modern baker goes to work in a more methodical way. To convert a sack of flour into bread the whole must be emptied into the trough, and partitioned off with a sprint board to suit the sponge required. Take twelve gallons of water heated to the required temperature (90°) and dissolve from ten to sixteen ounces of yeast, according to its strength, and mix it amongst the liquid for the sponge; dissolve 2lbs. of salt in the liquid and set a good, beaten, dry sponge. In the morning—or at such time as it is taken up—add six gallons of water with $1\frac{1}{2}$lbs. of salt broken well in the sponge; then make into dough.

The reader will notice that $\frac{1}{2}$lb. of salt more than the recognised quantity has been recommended, because, for myself, I prefer well-worked sponges, to obtain what flavour I can, and to keep, by the extra amount of salt, a pile on the bread.

All the following methods of sponging are adapted for either hand or machine doughing.

QUICK OR FLYING SPONGES.

These can be got ready sponged in from one to one and a half hours' time, according to the quality of the yeast and the temperature of the bakehouse. These points should always be kept in mind. After one sack of flour has been put into the trough make a sprint; add twelve gallons of water at about 100° F.; then dissolve in half a gallon of the sponge liquid 2lbs. of yeast (compressed yeast is here referred to), and set a weak sponge, about the consistency of sponge-cake batter; let this rise till you think it is ready; and then add 6 gallons of water at the same temperature as the sponge, with $3\frac{1}{2}$lbs. of salt dissolved in it; break well in and dough. This sponge, when thoroughly ready, requires quick, sharp manipulation in its removal to the oven. This method of working makes a really capital loaf.

OVERNIGHT SPONGING IN LARGE FIRMS.

For every one and a half pails, *i.e.*, about four and a half gallons of water, allow 5½oz. of yeast and 5½oz. of salt. Any required quantity may be set after this method, but it must be remembered that the larger the sponge the less yeast proportionately is needed—for instance, if for three pails 10oz. is used, for four and a half pails 14oz. is required, and so on. On taking up this sponge in the morning, for every pail and a half, or four and a half gallons, of water set in the sponge, one pail of water and 1lb. of salt must be allowed. Good bread by this, as by the last method, is made.

TO MAKE A FULL SPONGE WITH PARISIAN BARM, WITHOUT QUARTER OR FERMENT.

For a 40-stone batch, put 20 gallons of water at the required heat into the trough, and add 3 gallons of Parisian barm with 4lbs. of salt dissolved in the liquid. Make into a sponge—(see "Modern Method of Sponging")—and when ripe put to it 12 gallons of water at the requisite temperature, with 2¼lbs. of salt dissolved in part of the liquid; break well in, and make into dough.

HOW TO SET A SPONGE.

In large bread-making firms where the doughing machine is not used, two men, and sometimes three, are required to set a sponge. The following is the proper method: When the requisite quantity of flour is in the trough, or, in the trade vernacular, "when the trough is pitched," the heat of the water ascertained by the thermometer to be correct, and the salt and yeast added, the first man begins operations by drawing a quantity of the flour into the liquor, and his assistant starts mixing it. Then both men mix the loose flour and the liquor together, and the flour that remains to be taken in is added. Care is here necessary to see that no dry flour adheres to the bottom of the trough. When all the flour and liquor is thoroughly mixed, throw the sponge from one end of the trough to the other, so as to take up any slack sponge that may remain in it ; repeat this until you have both ends of the trough clear. Dust the top of the sponge with flour, and then throw the sides of the sponge into the middle, finishing this process by giving it a thorough good beating. This is done by placing both arms half-way through the sponge, keeping the hands nearly touching one another, lifting as much sponge in the arms as can conveniently be held, and throwing it to the back or side of the trough ; continue throwing from end to end of the trough till the sponge is nice and dry. You may now rub the sponge from your arms, and scrape down the sides and ends of the trough. Draw the scrapings into the centre, and finish by bringing the back part of the sponge to the front ; give the top a dust of flour, and rub the flat of the hands down between the sponge and the sides and ends of the trough. It should be noted that weak flours require tighter sponges than ordinary or strong flours.

This is the first important stage in the interesting process of making bread with compressed yeast.

HOW TO TREAT OVER-WROUGHT SPONGES.

The following is the system adopted by many bakers : Allow an extra half-pound of salt to every twenty stone of flour on taking up the sponge. Use all speed and every reasonable expedient to get the batch into the oven, and see that the oven is from six to ten degrees over the usual heat.

This method of working strong sponges is to check fermentation.

A method put forth by a new school of bakers—and one which to a *practical* baker seems altogether inconsistent with the rule of cause and effect—is to add more yeast to an already overworked sponge. I have repeatedly tested this method with small quantities of sponge, but obtained very unsatisfactory results. Our views on fermentation and bread making are steadily changing; but to place a healthy body with an unhealthy one and expect favourable results is, so far as we at present know, unreasonable and altogether opposed to scientific research.

A specific or antidote for over-worked sponges which I can recommend, and one which I have tested with good results, is as follows:—To every twenty stone of flour dissolve six ounces of carbonate of soda with the water and salt required to take the sponge up. This will improve both the taste and the bloom of the bread; but it will not—nor will any other method—make sour bread sweet.

THE MANIPULATION OF DOUGH.

HOW TO MAKE DOUGH BY HAND.

Let the operator who has charge of the dough-making department see that sufficient flour is put into the trough to take up all the sponge. This can easily be done by observing the quantity of sponge that is set, and the strength of the flour used. Avoid the happy-go-lucky method that is followed in some establishments in making dough by hand—that is, adding scoopful after scoopful of flour to get the dough the required size after it is half made, as the result of this practice is to waste time, to tire out the operators, and to produce dough finished in an untradesmanlike manner. After mixing the flour in the sponge, shake the whole mass thoroughly together, for on this shaking process depend the quality and the easy manipulation of the dough. When the lot is well shaken, and no scrappy parts remain, cut the dough from end to end of the trough—(see "Method of Cutting Dough")—and let each cut part be well spread before placing one on top of the other. By cutting and spreading it three times from one end of the trough to the other, the dough should be well made. By this process, and with efficient workmen, a batch of sixty stone of flour can easily be made into dough in fifteen minutes. When the dough is having the last turn before finishing, use a mixture of rice-flour and flour, in equal quantities, to dust the bottom of the trough with, so that the dough will lift freely when throwing it on to the table. Before starting to make the dough, the operator should rub his arms over with melted lard. This will give him more freedom of action, as the dough that adheres to his arms will then the more easily rub off.

To be a good dough-maker, one must know exactly what to do, and when and how to do it.

METHOD OF CUTTING DOUGH.

When it is found requisite to remove the dough from the trough, or when the dough is made by the hand in the trough, the operator will find it of great advantage to cut the dough in a slanting direction instead of in the old recognised manner, *viz.*, in a straight line. If the old, unsystematic style of cutting is adopted, the mass that the part is cut from soon overlaps and mixes again with the cut part, necessitating greater labour to remove the part that is cut than if it had been done obliquely. Although this is apparently a simple little wrinkle, it will really prove of great benefit to the baker when making or cutting dough from the trough; and where this method is not already adopted I would strongly urge my brother craftsmen to at least give it a trial, as it will save a great deal of labour, especially in large firms.

HOW TO WEIGH OFF A BATCH OF BREAD.

In large bakeries a weigher-off requires an assistant as cutter-out, and it is of the utmost importance that both men should be quick in perception and thoroughly practical, for on this department of the manufacture of bread depend, in a great measure, the profits that accrue to the employer.

The weigher-off takes the shell-plate of the scales between his thumb and fingers, the bottom of the plate resting on his fingers, with his thumb on the top, so that when the dough is placed upon it he will, if he has the lightness of touch requisite in a good weigher-off, know at once, by the pressure of the scale-plate on his thumb and fingers, if the dough requires adding to or taking from it. He should also be able to tell by the weight of the cut dough as he lifts it from the table to the scale-plate. The most important thing is to know exactly how much is required to make the dough the proper weight, and to make one motion of the hand finish the operation. That is, if the loaf is two ounces short of the weight required, the weigher must guess the quantity at once, and not put four ounces on when only two are required, as this entails a waste of time and is most untradesmanlike. The same applies when the dough is overweight. With two practical men at the scales, if the cutter-out is an expert at this part of his trade, weighing off dough becomes merely a matter of form, as the weight of the cut pieces has very seldom to be altered. Two such men can very easily keep two, and sometimes three others rolling up loaves of dough at their very quickest. A modern bakery of any size ought to have two or three good scalesmen, so as to accelerate the work and make the financial part of the business both accurate and reliable.*

HOW TO ROLL UP LOAVES OF DOUGH.

This is the first process the dough undergoes when the batch is being weighed off. Take in each hand one of the pieces weighed, keeping the cut or moist part of the dough lying on the table, and the scrappy or dry part, if any, towards the top. Then with the heel of each hand press the sides of the dough on the table, and with the fingers turn the sides into the centre; repeat this till each piece is round and the dough has a nice clear skin, and then draw the close of the dough into the centre underneath—the close will then be imperceptible. The rolled-up loaves are now placed on dusted boards holding from thirty to forty 2lb. loaves; the boards are then placed one on top of another, or run on shelves in a press made for the purpose, and left until the moulding process is begun.

Four ounces of flour and rice-flour, mixed in equal proportions, should be placed about sixteen inches from the front of the table, to keep the loaves dry while the baker is rolling them up. Two ounces of flour should also be placed at the same distance

---

* I have recently inspected a dough-divider, which is now coming into general use in large firms. This machine divides, at one operation, the required weight of dough into forty 2lb. loaves, and will prove a great boon in large businesses.

on the table in front of the baker to keep the loaves dry while moulding.

HOW TO MOULD A SQUARE LOAF.

After the dough has been brought through its various stages of fermentation, moulding a loaf is the next most difficult process in our trade. Take the dough firmly in your hands, making sure that the moist or "green" part, which is to be found on one side of the rolled-up loaves of dough, is next the table. This little wrinkle is requisite to secure a good skin. The closed part of the dough should be clear of the table, and is generally at the upper far part of the loaf. Commence by throwing the two sides into the centre of the loaf. Then draw the back part squarely into the centre, joining it with the heel of the hand, giving it a firm bash, and then rolling it with both hands into the half mould. The close of the loaf is now uppermost, with each side a little narrower than the centre. Then bash or press out the half-moulded loaf and throw the side parts over each other in the centre; again bash and close in. Closing in is done with 2lb. loaves by bringing the back part of the dough to the front part and firmly rolling the dough back. Then once more bring the two parts together, bashing or squeezing them, and at the same time squaring off the loaf. In moulding square loaves the body should have an easy movement. The manipulator must have the utmost command of his arms, at the same time keeping the loaf firmly in his hands during the whole process. By this method a nice square loaf can be made, having both the requisites of a well-moulded loaf, *viz.*, firmness and a nice silky skin. Some experts mould a loaf in each hand. This does very well for square tin loaves, but I do not approve of it for moulding square loaves for oven-bottom batches. Let a man be ever so clever or expert in moulding a square loaf with each hand, there is always a lack of firmness, texture, and artistic finish with this method of moulding. To mould a good loaf requires conception and practice.

HOW TO MOULD A ROUND LOAF.

Begin as for a square loaf, that is, by having your moist, or, in trade language, " green " part of the dough next to the table. Divide the dough into two parts, having the right hand piece smaller than the left. Now chaff this into two round pieces—(see " How to Roll up Loaves of Dough," chaffing being the same process, only more expeditious)—with a close in each part no larger than a pigeon's eye. Place the two closes together; then bash the loaf with the heel of the right hand, and press the elbow of the right arm into the centre of the loaf, and your moulding process is finished. This, like the preceding style for moulding square loaves, requires practice and strength to mould the loaves firm, and to give them a silky and suitable texture. Learners should try to properly half mould first, leaving the finish of the loaf to those more able to accomplish the art.

MOULDING AND BOARDING.

Until very recently no machine had been invented to take the place of hand moulding,* and as it is not in general use it is

---

* A machine for moulding loaves has recently been invented by Mr. F. Westerman, of Chicago. It is claimed that the bread moulded by this machine is superior in texture to that moulded by hand. Be this as it may, from the illustration of the machine recently to hand it appears very intricate and complicated and to all appearance too expensive to come into general use. It may be of use in large firms; but I am afraid that the cleaning that must be required, and the difficulty of keeping the dough free from oil and grease, will also prove great drawbacks. However, it is the first practical attempt that has shown any likelihood of usefulness in this department of the trade, and I hope that the claims of the inventor may be verified.

very requisite for the foreman to see that the man he engages or recommends is a good moulder, as it is on the manner in which his work is done that a great deal of the success expected from the ovenman depends.

If the dough is of the ordinary consistency, the moulder should be able to finish his loaf in a quick, tradesmanlike manner; and the loaf, if square oven-bottom batch, should *be* square and firm; the skin, likewise, of the loaf should be smooth and silky, not cracked and soft, with long stringy marks here and there on the surface, or, as it often is, bazen-looking and rough. There is as much skill required in moulding a loaf well as in any hand labour in baking I know of.

If there are one or two moulding who throw up their finished loaves to the boarder in a soft state, this proof of their want of skill is soon discovered by either the setter-up or ovenman, who as a rule are not slow in letting the moulder's inefficiency be known in the proper quarter. And the ovenman is only doing his duty in thus protecting himself and his employer. Where two or three loaves are run at a time, it is annoying, to say the least of it, for him to see two good, firm loaves and one unfinished one on the same peel the bad one most likely running on to the oven bottom before he can get them into the course. Nor is he able to make his batch as square as it should be, as loaves moulded in this way throw him, as they say, "off his course." The same thing applies in the case of round or cottage bread—with this difference, that cottage dough should be tighter, and the deficiency is not so apparent. It does not matter so much for pan bread so long as it has a finished appearance and good skin, as the dough, after being put into the tins, is not handled till baked. Still, for long pans, to bring out a good, showy loaf with a nice pile, the loaf must be well moulded.

I have boarded for men who were moulding a cottage batch, and have actually seen the loaf with the close on the top, side, or anywhere but where it ought to be. Such experiences are, of course, exceptions; but the proper methods cannot be driven into men who have not the perception to see their utility. A man must be very expert before he can become a good boarder. In a modern bakery there are so many men allowed for each boarder that all his knowledge and energy are needed to keep the table clear. As the finished loaves come up he has to arrange them in rows of eight or nine, sides uppermost. Every third loaf is greased before being put on to the board, and they are arranged in rows to fit it; as each row is completed, the front ends of all the loaves in that row are greased, and so on till the board is filled. Next the tops of the loaves are docked, and they are put away in their places till the batch is moulded. At a given time the ovenman sees that the ovens are schuffled out, and up-sets are in their places round the oven. He begins to run the batch, usually eighteen or twenty 4lbs. in a course, or twenty-four to twenty-six 2lbs. And it is very interesting for an outsider, or one not belonging to the baking trade, to see how skilfully and speedily some bakers can arrange the loaves.

Round or cottage bread is easier to board and run than square batches. A considerable amount of practice is necessary before proficiency can be obtained in this part of the baking trade.

SETTING OR RUNNING BATCHES.

A good ovenman has always a certain amount of deference shown him in a modern bakery, and this is not to be wondered at when we think how much the quality and ultimate appearance of the bread depend on his knowledge and skill. It is painful to see a man working at an oven whose proper occupation would be grooming horses or working in a brick-field. Employers who are not practical men cannot imagine how much against their own interests it is to engage such. A batch of bread put into an evenly heated oven depends in a great measure for its flavour and weight on the dexterity of the baker. If, for instance, ten to fifteen minutes are required to set an ovenful of loaves—or, as we should say in trade parlance, a batch of bread —and the same time to draw them, then the first course of loaves put into the oven is consequently from twenty to thirty minutes longer baking than the last peelful put in. Thus the first two or three courses are more or less overbaked, and the weight of the first will be less than the last, as there is less moisture, and naturally less substance. Besides this, the loaf cuts in a crumbly fashion, and is dry to eat and deficient of that nice, mellow, glutenous taste and nutty flavour characteristic of a good loaf. It will thus be seen that it behoves employers to secure good, active, skilful ovenmen to turn out bread that will please the eye and gratify the palate.

To secure an equal baking in running a batch of pan bread into the oven, no great skill or extraordinary art is required; only speed. I have repeatedly run 180 4lb. tin loaves into the oven in two minutes and a half, and filled three ovens with 180 4lb. loaves each in eight minutes, two handing forward and one peeling on. This of course was not our usual time, and was only done, so to speak, out of bravado, to ascertain in what time it really could be done. But though it is an easy matter for an ordinary baker of some celerity to run a batch of tin bread, the running of an oven-bottom batch of square, round, or cottage loaves is quite another thing. To ensure success with these a man must be an expert in the handling of the peel, and must have a quick eye, a steady hand, and quick perceptions all round. For a man of this stamp it is essential to have an assistant who is a good setter-up, *i.e.*, one who squares up the loaves and prepares them for the ovenman, or puts them on the peel ready for the oven. In Glasgow, where they are in great request, such men are paid really good wages.

PLAIN AND FANCY BREAD, ETC.

The common bread of Great Britain, or bread for general use, may be divided into three classes : (1) Wheaten bread, made of the very finest flour and generally called "firsts"; (2) Household bread, made of somewhat coarser flour and usually called "seconds;" and (3) Brown bread, made in various qualities.

The finest flour is entirely separated from the bran or husks; the second is not thoroughly so; while from the coarsest flour the broad bran only is removed.

Coarse bread, made from what the Scotch called overhead flour, was formerly much used in Scotland. This quality of bread had a nice, nutty flavour. It can be made by the same method as given for the manufacture of full sponges.

Brown bread is admitted to be our lowest class of bread. The baker has also so many chances of adulterating it, though I do not say this is always done.

Competition in the making of bread is now so keen that a practical baker is sometimes at his wit's end to produce a loaf that will be at once agreeable to the taste and pleasing to the eye. But he is still not so sorely handicapped in the race and struggle for trade and custom as the outsiders who follow the commercial pursuit of supplying bread to the masses. I here allude to bread companies, stores, grocers, and other dealers who make and sell bread—the two latter sometimes selling at a loss, in order to advertise their other commodities.

The first-named—the bread companies—we can partly tolerate, as in many cases a certain amount of the profit is shared with the employees; and, to judge by the signs of the times, we may expect that the bulk of the baking trade will eventually fall into their hands. This would be a boon to journeymen; but till such a time comes let the trade protect industrial effort in a reasonable manner, so as not to clog the interests of employers or employed.

Grocers and other dealers have not the same chance of success in dressing their shop windows with nice, clean, showy bread as a modern practical baker has. I have seen bread jumbled anyhow and anywhere, amongst paraffin oil, matches, soap, candles, and even blacking. How tempting to a customer such a display must be! This shows that a real baker has a great advantage over a make-believe one, who, instead of sticking to the occupation fate has chosen for him, goes poaching about, and, figuratively speaking, poking his finger into everybody's pie and filching a piece out of every dish he sets his eyes upon, unmindful of the harm such selfish action causes to practical tradesmen. Happily, such individuals often get their fingers burnt, but that does not deter others from following the same selfish course.

I now propose to describe a class of bread which is second to none in the market. The following are my methods of preparation, as adapted to the requirements of the establishment in which I am engaged. Anyone properly attending to the instructions here given will be well pleased with the results; there are no better or more expeditious methods known to the trade.

VIENNA BREAD.

This I claim to be our highest grade of white bread, and one not affording opportunities for adulteration.

Take 8lbs. of flour (Hungarian best brand), three quarts of milk and water in equal proportions, 3½oz. of compressed yeast, and 1½oz. of salt. Mix the water (warm) with the milk so that the final temperature may be about 85° F.; dissolve the yeast in this, and with a little of the flour make a flour ferment, which should stand for about one hour; then add the remainder of the flour and the salt, and thoroughly knead all together. Let this lie for two hours and a half, and work off, prove, and bake. If a jet of steam can be introduced into the oven the bread will get nicely glazed.

FANCY COTTAGE LOAVES.

This class of bread, and the fancy kinds following, must be sponged with Hungarian flour, and doughed with it also. "P.W.M." is a suitable brand. Machine the dough to a good stiffness in the mixer; let it lie to prove for an hour and a half, and then throw it upon the table and weigh off at 1¼lb., if for cottages, to sell at threepence each. Roll the loaves up into boards, using a little rice flour for dusting and rolling up; after all are worked up cover with either boards or sacks; prove one hour and start to mould. Split each piece of dough into two parts, one considerably larger than the other; mould separately with a fine, silky skin, and place the smaller part upon the larger; punch with the palm of your hand, and dig your elbow into the centre of the loaf; place on boards a little distance apart, egg over the top, and prove in proving press. Do not prove them too much, or they will fall in the oven. When ready wash again with egg, and run two at a time on the oven bottom, just allowing them to touch and no more. The oven is in the best condition for baking these just after a tin batch has been turned out. This method, if properly adhered to, should afford satisfaction.

HOW TO MAKE TWISTS.

Weigh off at 1lb. 6oz. for threepence. Go through the same process as for cottages. When the dough is ready to work off divide each piece into three equal parts, and roll each part out to a length of four or five inches. When this has been done, again roll out each part about fourteen inches long, tapering at the ends and thickening in the middle; now attach the three pieces to each other, end to end; then plait, as it were, the side pieces round the centre one till the twist is complete, tapering at the ends as before; place on sheet tins and egg over the top; prove as before, and again egg. Bake them in the same kind of oven as for cottages.

COBURGS, OR COBS,

make a fine, showy line when nicely got up, and look well in a shop window. Weigh off the required quantity from cottage dough and prove for the same time on boards. After they are rolled up as for cottages, take one in each hand and mould round to a fine, silky skin; place on boards a little apart; wash over with water and prove. The time for proving must be left to the operator's practical judgment, for much depends on the heat of the prover, the ripeness of the sponge, and the temperature of the bakehouse. When ready, wash over with water again; then with a sharp knife cut across the middle to the depth of one inch, and again at right angles to form a cross; run them on to the oven bottom, a little apart; keep the door closed for twenty minutes, and bake them to a deep, golden brown. Weigh at 1lb. 10oz. for threepence. When these loaves are got up to perfection they are crusty all round, and have the appearance of a full-blown rose.

COMMON VIENNA LOAVES.

Prepare dough as for cottages. Mould the loaf nice and firm, making it square and about twelve inches long, and properly finish it. Cut the top of the loaf, just breaking the skin of the dough, from end to end; then cross-wise from opposite corners. Place on tins, egg them over, and prove. When ready, egg over again and bake in a nice heat. Weigh at 1lb. 8oz. for fourpence.

MELVIN LOAVES.

The dough used for these should be a shade slacker than that used for the above, but not as slack as for tin dough. Proceed as for cottages; then mould the dough up round, not forgetting to have a fine skin on the loaf at the finish. Egg the loaf all over, and with a knife mark all round from bottom to top; then reverse the cutting to form a diamond shape. Place on sheet tins and cover with the Melvin tins; prove, and bake in a good oven. Weigh at 1lb. 10oz. for fourpence.

By practice alone can one tell when these loaves are proved enough, as they cannot be seen when once put to prove. My method is to knock the tins with the knuckles; in a short time you will get to know the difference of sound, as the loaf rises and gradually fills the tin in proving.

SANDWICH LOAVES.

This is another nice line, and will greatly help a display in the window. Hungarian flour is used in doughing and sponging, but the dough must be very much slacker than for cottages, as that used for these loaves is technically known as tin dough. Clean your tins, and then slightly grease them. The common size is $3\frac{1}{2}$lbs. for sixpence, or 7lbs. for a shilling. But, of course, the weight of all these loaves is regulated by the price of the flour. Less time for proving will be required than for cottages, as this dough, being of a softer nature, sooner matures. Fill your tins at above weights; prove, and bake in a rather brisk oven.

FRENCH LOAVES

are made from the same kind of dough as sandwich loaves, weighed at 4lbs. and 2lbs. each. When proved, a flat piece of sheet iron or a flat scraper is used to cut the dough across the middle of the longest part of the loaf; press the scraper or cutter down through the dough, touching the bottom of the tin. As soon after cutting as possible put the loaves into the oven so that the cut just made may not join up again; the loaf will then leave the oven with a nice incision in the centre. This class, when properly got up, looks well. One penny more per 4lb. loaf is charged than for the ordinary fine loaf. It is well worth it.

BOX ROLLS.

Use the dough as for sandwich loaves, proceeding in the same way. Weigh off at $1\frac{3}{4}$lb. for threepence, or $3\frac{1}{2}$lbs. for sixpence; prove, and bake in a sharp oven. The tins used must be square, and fitted in size to the above weights. An ordinary

2lb. or 4lb. tin will not do. The operator should bear in mind that Hungarian flour, prepared according to my instructions, will take a higher bloom and appear more " topy," as our technical friends phrase it, if baked in an oven of the same temperature as is used for ordinary bread.

PULLED BREAD.

Take a new-baked loaf, and, either with the fingers or a large fork, pull the inside into pieces about the size of an egg ; place them on a clean sheet tin, and bake in a sound oven. When baked let the pieces be of a nice brown colour, and as dry and crumpy as rusks. Pulled bread is sold at one shilling per pound, and is mostly used in large hotels.

SODA BREAD.

Eight pounds of flour (Hungarian), 3oz. of tartar, 2oz. of soda, 2oz. of salt. Sift through the sieve; make a bay in the flour, and dough with buttermilk. Make a nice working dough, and weigh off at 1¾lb. for threepence. Put on a flat sheet tin, egg on top, place round tins over, and bake.

AERATED BREAD.

Properly speaking, this is a substitute for aerated bread, as the baker has not the mechanical appliances for forcing the gas into the dough, as in aerated bread. The following is the method : For every pound of Hungarian flour use a bottle or gill of aerated soda-water, and allow salt at the rate of two ounces to the stone, which will only be a small pinch to a pound. Empty the soda-water into a basin ; as quickly as possible throw flour upon it; mix and get as much gas as you can, and in a few minutes put it into the oven. This is not so showy as the original aerated bread, and the reason is obvious. The soda-water should be as brisk as possible.

PATENT OR UNLEAVENED BREAD.

Twenty pounds of Hungarian flour, 8oz. of cream of tartar, 5oz. of soda, 1lb. of lard, 1lb. of sugar, and 6oz. of salt. Dough with churned milk into a nice-sized dough. Weigh at $1\frac{3}{4}$lb. for threepence. Grease each loaf all round, and put four into a pan made for the purpose, with a fitting lid. The pan should be thirteen inches in diameter and seven inches deep. When these are baked they should be nice, showy, three-cornered loaves.

HOME-MADE BREAD.

Put one stone of flour in a pan or basin; dissolve two ounces of good yeast in a gill and a half of warm water, and place them in a hole made in the centre of the flour. Stir about four ounces of flour amongst the yeast and water and let it rise in a warm place. When it is ready, which will be when it has a nice cauliflower-like head, dissolve two ounces of salt in a tea-cup of warm water, and pour it upon the ferment. Proceed to add as much flour as may be requisite to make all into a nice dough, and put it in a warm place to rise. When risen, divide it into the required sizes and bake the dough in tins, giving it a slight proof first. It would be as well for bakers to remember that half an ounce of salt is required for a four-pound loaf. Different classes of flour require more, but this is the average.

FAMILY, OR HOME-BAKED BREAD, MADE WITH BREWERS' BARM.

An expeditious and simple method of making bread for a small family, or for wholesale bakers who supply home-made bread, is as follows :—

Put a bushel of flour, all but four pounds, into a tub or pan, and in winter warm it near the fire or oven. Take a pint of good, fresh brewers' barm, with a small quantity of warm water; pour the water and yeast gently into a hole in the middle of the flour, mix the water and yeast with sufficient flour to make it into a stiff batter, and cover it up in a warm place till it has risen. Then dissolve in warm water six ounces of salt, and add it to the batter with sufficient water to make all into a nice mellow dough. After it has again risen make it into loaves, giving it a slight proof, and bake in a good oven.

I may here observe that practice and sound judgment are needed to properly regulate the heat of the oven. Dough that is going too freely requires a sharper oven than ordinary dough. Pan or tin loaves requiring proving should have a good sharp oven, both to check the fermentation and impart flavour to the bread. Cold ovens are useless for bread baking, for bread thus baked looks boiled, and always has a bad flavour.

NAMES OF VARIOUS LOAVES MADE IN BRITAIN.

Firstly, there is 4lb. batch, square and round; then 2lb. batch, square and round—although the round is called cottage in some districts. Further, there are pan or tin loaves; sandwich, square and round, from $1\frac{1}{2}$lb. to 14lbs.; French, twist and Vienna loaves; Coburg loaves, cobs, and cottages; the heart loaves in Edinburgh called French; Melvins, crusty and crumby loaves, tin cakes, Hungarian loaves, and others. The most popular of these have, I think, been enumerated.

HOT ROLLS IN ENGLAND.

Rolls are not in such great demand in England as in Scotland, owing, I suppose, to the fact that the English housewife is able to make so many different tit-bits and choice morsels for her own table. It is a notable fact that, with the exception of those working in our large centres of population, very few bakers in England make rolls—at any rate, very few in comparison with the quantity sold in Scotland. French rolls are mostly used here; they are weighed at various weights, and halved, chaffed, and stented out—*i.e.*, made sharp or pointed at the ends; placed on French roll tins; proved, and baked in a sharp oven. They must be well baked, or they will not rasp as all French rolls should.

Next are plain rolls, moulded up square and placed in rows on edged tins; each course is greased at the ends, so that they may readily separate after they are baked. They are worked off in this manner, proved, and baked.

Cob rolls also are weighed at various weights, the dough being a little tighter than for plain or French rolls; they are chaffed up round, and one part placed on the top of the other, the uppermost being the smallest, and the thumb is pressed into them to hold them together. They are either placed on tins, proved, and baked on the tins; or placed on warm boards, proved, and run on the oven bottom.

In some watering places during the season when visitors are present, it is becoming common to order from the baker rolls of different varieties, such as horse-shoes, twists, turnovers, cobs, and Jews' loaves, entailing an extraordinary amount of labour on the baker, and causing him to waste precious time—which he can ill afford to do at that time of the year.

SCOTCH ROLLS.

Ah! Scotland is the place where rolls *par excellence* can be obtained, from the diminutive loaf, top and bottom, to the large penny "swine," a large roll which was first chaffed, then stented, placed on a warm board to prove, and dusted with flour before being run into the oven. It had another name—"Penny Dag." I have sold them under the name of "Coarse Geordies," but this was in the south of Scotland, and people's tastes in names may have altered. The majority of bakers in Scotland do a fair trade in rolls. Scotchmen are like Americans—they like hot bread: whether it is from the coldness of the climate or a natural taste is a matter for conjecture; but the fact remains that they like rolls, especially hot ones. In ordinary shops the roll dough is taken from the sponge in the morning before the extra water is added; or enough is taken from the sponge water at night during the sponging, and set in a somewhat warmer place (either at the trough end, or in a boat or tub for the purpose), as the sponge must be well worked for rolls. In firms where a large quantity is made a separate sponge is set for them. There are baps, long rolls, round, plain, cottages, etc. They are made as follows: After the dough is headed up, as it is called, the rolls are weighed off. Each man then takes a weighed-off portion, halves it, takes the parts one in either hand, and chaffs them—either long or round. Let us take the long first. The boards on which they are proved should fit the oven. While a boy is beating the boards a man starts to stent them out; the boards are then dusted with a mixture of rice flour and flour, and the rolls are placed on them in rows, touching each other, but with the ends at least one inch apart. They are put aside to prove as each board is filled; when proved, which should take from half to three-quarters of an hour, each row is cut in two, or through the middle. The oven man then takes them carefully and quickly in his hand and places them on the peel, and then runs them on the oven bottom. But he must be careful in lifting not to knock the proof out of them.

PLAIN ROUND ROLLS are chaffed round, placed touching one another on an edge pan, proved, and baked.

BAPS is the name given to rolls peculiar to some districts. They are chaffed up like long rolls, but in stenting they are knocked out flat with the hand, placed on warm boards, then cut in the centre with a sharp knife, washed on the top and put apart to prove. They are baked on the oven bottom.

There are a good many Glasgow scones, as they are called, that come under the head of rolls, but as this book treats on bread exclusively they must be omitted.

BROWN BREAD, WHEAT MEAL, RYE, ETC.

The brown bread craze I take to be exploded; if I could have my own way I would see that those who advocate the feeding of the masses on brown bread were fed on it themselves, until they should exclaim "Hold! enough!" We should hear less then of the benefits of brown bread. That it suits some constitutions better than white I do not for a moment doubt or deny; let those whom it suits stick to their brown bread, just as some affect vegetables and despise beef. But to enable men to stand the strain of physical labour or excessive brain work, I strongly recommend good, wholesome, well-made white bread. I am sure that the inhabitants of Great Britain would compare favourably as regards strength or endurance with the much-lauded ancients, who are supposed to have lived entirely on brown bread or crushed wheat. Take, for instance, Captain Nares's expedition to the North Pole. Can we refer to any better test of strength and endurance than was there displayed? They were not fed on brown bread, but on unleavened, hard, white bread. Going to the other extreme for another instance, look at our own soldiers in the Soudan—what extremes of heat and fatigue they were subjected to in the burning, thirsty desert! They were not fed on brown bread; and I say again that the notion of the support derived from brown bread is an exploded theory, and its upholders cannot prove their position either scientifically or argumentatively. If these people are asked upon what grounds they support and base the use of wheat-meal and brown bread, they probably reply that the most nutritious part of the wheat is thrown away when the bran is rejected. Now, really, if one may be allowed to say so, this is all bosh. For this reason: there are several skins covering the nutritive part of the bran, which actually pass through the body undigested. We have in Dr. Graham a good authority on this subject. Professor Jago likewise speaks in no uncertain voice upon the fallacy of the brown bread theory.

In a little manual of Grecian antiquities, giving an account of the manners and customs of the ancient Greeks, we have the following extract on bread: "Bread, termed Aρτος, and by metonymy Σιτος, was their principal food; hence this word denotes sometimes all sorts of meat and drink. But the chief attention of the Greeks was confined to the Aρτος, wheat bread, and to the μαζα, barley bread. In the composition of the latter they sometimes used oil."*

---

* "A Manual of Grecian Antiquities, being a compendious account of the manners and customs of the Ancient Greeks, etc.," by G. H. Smith. London: Published by John R. Priestly, 1832. Page 211.

They did this, no doubt, because they knew no other method either of making the bread or of preparing the grain. The Greeks, highly civilised as they were, had nothing like the knowledge we possess. They did not use machinery at all like ours, even in the most rudimentary state, for properly converting grain into flour. A great many people lose sight of the fact that our milling industry has grown bit by bit from the ancients' crude manner of grinding corn down to the latest improvements of modern times. Why do not the supporters of brown or wheat-meal bread put forward the ancient manner of baking as an argument in support of the same, *viz.*, baking under ashes, on the hearth, or in an earthen or iron pan?

In concluding these brief remarks on brown and wheat-meal bread, I give an abstract from Professor Jago's views on the matter. He says : " The whole meal and flour from which the bran and germs have not been removed do not keep well. These bodies contain oil and nitrogenous principles which readily decompose, producing rancidity and mustiness in flavour. Not only do the changes occur in the flour, but they also proceed apace in the dough. The diastic bodies of the bran and germ attack the starch, and more or less convert it into dextrine and maltose; they further attack the gluten, that remarkably elastic body which confers on wheaten flour alone of all the cereals the power of forming a light, spongy, well-risen loaf. The gluten, under the action of the bran and germ, loses its elasticity, and becomes fragile and incapable of retaining the gas produced during fermentation: the result is heavy, sodden, indigestible bread."

WHEAT-MEAL BREAD.

Granulated wheat meal is superior to rough or whole wheat meal, as it most nearly approaches our modern fine flour.

Dissolve 2½oz. of compressed or German yeast and 2½oz. of salt in one gallon of water of the required heat; make this into a nice dry sponge, and in the morning, or when taken up, add three quarts of water—heated according to the state of the sponge—and 5oz. of salt, and make them lightly into a dough. When it is proved, weigh off for loaves the required size; again prove, and bake. I find from experience that brown flours, of all grades of quality, are best worked up as lightly as possible, and baked with less heat than is necessary for flours of finer quality.

RYE BREAD

is best made from the fine sponge. After breaking-in your sponge in the morning make a bay on the table with as much rye flour as may be required. Put as much of the sponge into the bay as will take up all the flour—or meal, as it is called. Dry it up as well as possible, for it is of a very sticky nature; then proceed in the same manner as for wheat-meal bread.

Rye flour and barley meal flour mixed in equal quantities are sometimes used for the manufacture of rye bread. It is baked in 4lb., 6lb. and 8lb. loaves. This bread is generally set in the afternoon, so as to be ready to be put in the oven the last thing at night and taken out the first thing in the morning, as a great deal of soaking is required. Put one stone of the above mixture of rye and barley flour into a pan; make a hole in the middle of the flour, and pour into it a good gill of warm water containing 2oz. of German or compressed yeast. Mix a little flour with the liquid, to make a nice soft paste; dust a little flour over the top, and put it in a warm place to ferment. It will not rise much, but will break through the flour on the top: when it is considered ready, put in as much warm water as will take in all the flour, and make into a nice-sized dough. This should be set apart to rise—it should rise to some extent in the dough. Add to the above-mentioned water 2½oz. of salt. When you think the mixture is ready, it may be put into the tins to be proved, and then baked overnight.

BROWN-BREAD MEAL.

A well-known baker in the north has lately introduced a brown-bread meal which is a blending of certain cereals. Having worked it, I can safely say it is as near perfection as any of this class. The method of working it is the same as that here given for wheat meal. This particular flour is prepared by Messrs. Seatree, of Penrith and Liverpool.

MASLEN BREAD.

This bread is very nourishing, and good for those who like it. The bread is made from a mixture of wheat meal and rye meal blended together in equal quantities, and called maslen meal. To every stone of this meal use 4oz. of lard. Place the flour on the table, then make a hole or bay in the centre, and rub the lard with a little of the flour in the centre of the bay. When the sponge that has been set from fine flour has had its quantity of water and salt added and broken in, take as much of the sponge as will use up the full 14lbs., and place it in the bay or hole made in the flour, making the dough the same size as for ordinary brown bread. Give it the usual time to prove; then weigh off at 1lb. 12oz. for threepence, prove, and bake in a moderate oven. It can either be baked in square tins in the usual manner, or the dough can be placed in oval tins and turned on to a sheet tin, and then proved. This makes the loaf look more fancy, but in using these oval tins, for any kind of bread, and proving and baking by the above method, care should be taken that an air-hole is left in the top of the tin, otherwise the loaf will not rise or appear tradesmanlike when baked. When there is no air-hole in the tin, the likelihood is that the heat of the oven will force the dough out of the bottom of the tin, spoiling what would otherwise be a nice showy loaf. The cause of this is that the steam generated from the moist dough collects in the space between the dough and the upper part of the tin, and when there is no air hole it naturally forces its way out at the weakest part, carrying the dough along with it. The weakest part in this case is round the bottom rim of the loaf-tin, that is, between the rim and the flat surface of the sheet tin.

AERATED MALT BREAD.

This is an excellent bread, which acts both as a tonic and a mild laxative. Weigh 8lbs. of granulated wheat meal, 3oz. of cream of tartar, and 2oz. of carbonate of soda. Sift all these ingredients three times through the sieve, make a bay in the centre of the meal, and add 8oz. of malto-peptone extract, 1¾oz. of salt, and nearly half a gallon of fresh buttermilk. Dissolve the salt and malt extract in the milk, then make into a nice-sized dough. Weigh off at 1¾lb., mould them oval, and place in dusted oval tins; then turn them on to a large sheet tin, and bake in a sound oven. These are sold at fourpence each.

FERMENTED MALT BREAD,

or malt bread made from the morning's sponge after the sponge has had its required salt and water added, and been thoroughly broken in. To every gallon of this sponge use 8oz. of malto-peptone extract (or common malt extract), and 8oz. of lentil flour. Mix all these ingredients together, and then use sufficient granulated wheat meal to make the whole into a nice-sized dough. Let it prove, and work off as for aerated malt bread; then prove them again in the tins. When ready, bake in a sound oven. Weight and price as aerated malt bread.

GERM BREAD

is also a very good bread, taken in conjunction with brown. Dissolve ½oz. of yeast in fully one quart of water, then mix in the water 3½lbs. of germ flour, and let it start fermenting. Put into tins, prove, and bake.

I have been informed that Mr. Smith, the patentee of this flour, mixes 3lbs. of salt with every twenty stone of germ flour, therefore no salt need be added.

DIET, OR WHEAT-MEAL BREAD, UNFERMENTED.

Take 12lbs. of rough wheat meal, 6oz. of cream of tartar, and 3oz. of soda. Sift these through the sieve, make a bay in the flour, and add 6oz. of castor sugar and 3oz. of salt. Mix all together with buttermilk, and make into a nice dough, weighing off at 2lbs. for fourpence. Bake on the oven bottom, with oval tins placed over them on the peel. Put into the oven as soon after doughing as possible.

SUBSTITUTES FOR WHEAT BREAD.

Corn, of which bread is made in this and other civilised countries, comprehends the seeds of all ceralia, or farinaceous grass-like plants, for they all contain a farinaceous or mealy substance of a like nature, which substance is chiefly composed of starch. The seeds or grain in common use are firstly and principally wheat, rye, and barley.

Wheat is the only grain from which really good porous or light bread can be made; but rye and barley are occasionally used, as well as other grain. Such bread, however, is of an inferior quality. A sort of bread is made from oats, maize, rice, millet, etc. Rice is said, no doubt truly, to nourish more human beings than all the other seeds which are used for food put together; and it is considered by many to be the most nutritive of all kinds of grain. Accum, in "The Art of Making Bread," says: "It has been ascertained that one part of rice contains as much food and useful nourishment as six of wheat." This, by the way, is an assertion I am much inclined to disbelieve. However, there is no doubt that rice makes a very nourishing, healthy food, notwithstanding the prejudices that prevailed against it on account of the unfounded allegation that it caused eye diseases. Rice is the principal food of eastern nations, a fact that shows that it is not unhealthy. Rice is not often made into bread without flour, and when it is, it forms a loaf of very inferior quality.

Maize is frequently employed as bread-corn in America, but it will not of itself make good loaf bread. Unleavened cakes are made of it, however, which are both nutritive and palatable.

Oatmeal is seldom used for loaf-bread, but it makes an excellent unleavened bread, and is much eaten in Scotland, Lancashire, and several northern counties. It is made into thin cakes called oatcake, and preferred by many to wheaten bread.

BREAD MADE FROM ROOTS.

M. Parmentier, at one time chief apothecary in the *Hôtel des Invalides*, has published numerous and very curious experiments on the vegetables which in times of scarcity might be used for the support of animals, instead of ordinary food. The result of these experiments, in the mind of M. Parmentier, was that starch is the nutritive part of farinaceous vegetables; and the farina of plants was identical with the starch of wheat. The plants from which he extracted the farina are Bryony, the Iris, the Gladiolus, Ranunculus, Fumaria, Arum, and Dracunculus, the Mandragora, Colchicum, Filipendula, Helleborus, and the roots of the *gramen canum arvense*, or dog grass of the fields. The following is the mode employed by M. Parmentier to extract the starch, or farina from these vegetables: the roots are cleaned and scraped, then bruised and boiled and afterwards reduced to pulp, which being soaked in a considerable quantity of water, deposits a white sediment; this, when properly washed and dried, will be found to be pure starch. M. Parmentier converted this starch into bread by mingling it with an equal quantity of potatoes, reduced to a pulp, and employing the usual quantity of yeast, or other leaven. The bread, I am informed, had no bad taste, and was of excellent quality. From these experiments of M. Parmentier it appears that it is chiefly the amylaceous matter, or starch of grain, that is nutritious; and that the nutritive quality of other vegetable substances depends in a great measure on the quantity of that matter which they contain. Starch formed into a jelly and diffused in water will keep a long time without change.

APPLE BREAD

is a bread said to be very superior to potato bread, and has been made from common apples with meal. Boil one-third of peeled apples; while quite warm bruise them into two-thirds of flour, including the proper quantity of leaven, or yeast; knead without water, the fruit juice being quite sufficient. When this mixture has acquired the consistency of paste, put it into a vessel to rise for about twelve hours. By this process very sweet bread is obtained.

MESLIN BREAD.

An excellent bread can be made from what is called meslin. Meslin is a mixture of rye and wheat, raised, or grown, on the same ground at the same time, and reaped, thrashed, ground and dressed in a mixed state.

RAGWORT BREAD.

In times of scarcity bread has been made from the roots of this plant. When ragwort root is first taken out of the ground it is soft and viscous, but it soon becomes hard, and may be kept in that state for years without at all deteriorating, providing it is kept in a dry, airy place. When the root is ground and reduced to flour, which is easily done, it has an agreeable nut-like taste. It is said to be easily digested when made into bread, and to be more nutritive and "exhilarating" than wheat bread. The same properties and effects are said to be found in radishes; but I am incredulous in the matter.

TURNIP BREAD

is made by mixing turnips in equal quantities with flour. The turnips must be first cleaned, then pared and boiled; wash them and press the water out of them—at least, the greater part; mix with an equal weight of coarse meal flour, and make the dough in the usual manner. When risen, form into loaves, and bake rather longer than for ordinary bread. It will be light and sweet when taken from the oven, with a little taste of the turnip. After being allowed to stand for twelve hours, according to one authority, the taste of the turnip is scarcely perceptible, and the smell is quite gone; after twenty-four hours it would not be known that turnips are in its composition, although it still has a peculiar sweet taste. It appears to be rather superior to bread made of wheat flour only, is fresher and moister, and even after a week continues to be very good. I think, however, it cannot be so good as wheat bread, for, independently of other considerations, turnips do not contain so much starch or nutritive matter as wheat.

SALEP BREAD.

Dr. Percival recommends the employment of orchis root in powder, or, as it is called, salep. He says that an ounce of salep, dissolved in a quart of water and mixed with two pounds of flour, two ounces of yeast, and eighty grains of salt, produced a remarkably good loaf, weighing 3lbs. 2oz; while a loaf made of an equal quantity of the other ingredients, without salep, weighed but 2lbs. 12oz. If the salep be in too great quantities its peculiar taste will be distinguishable in the bread.

OAT AND BARLEY BREAD.

The Norwegians, we are informed, make bread of barley and oatmeal grown together. This bread, it is added, improves by age, and may be kept thirty to forty years. At their great festivals they use their oldest bread, and it is not unusual at the baptism of a child to have bread that was baked at the baptism of its grandfather. It is made in extremely thin cakes like oatcake, but much larger, and is baked on a sort of " back stone," an open flat plate of iron, under which is the fire. It is always made by women.

DEBRETZEN BREAD.

In some parts of Hungary, Debretzen for instance, they have a peculiar mode of fermenting bread without yeast, by means of a leaven made as follows: Two large handfuls of hops are boiled in four quarts of water; this decoction is poured upon as much wheaten bran as it will moisten, and 4lbs. or 5lbs. of leaven is added. When the mass is warm the ingredients are well worked together, so as to be thoroughly mixed; it is then deposited in a warm place for twenty-four hours, and afterwards divided into small pieces about the size of hens' eggs, which are dried by being placed upon a board and exposed to dry air, but not to the sun. When dry, they are laid up for use, and may be kept for six months.

BREAD A HUNDRED YEARS OLD.

The keeper of the archives for the Hungarian county Marmaros found lately stowed away with some ancient registers a packet bearing this inscription: " Qualitas panis Marmatici in penuria A.D. 1786." (Quality of the bread of Marmaros in the year of want 1786.) The bread is partly composed of oatmeal, but the greater portion of it is the bark of trees. I believe the county authorities have directed the specimen to be preserved in the local museum.

OVENS.

Among the earliest authentic records we possess of bread ovens, are those of the ancient Greeks; and it is a matter for some surprise that they, so far advanced in art, refinement, and culture, should have for any considerable time retained their rude mode of bread baking. If we take into a moment's consideration the beauty of their exquisitely designed porticoes, theatres, forums, and gymnasia—if we think of the temple of Diana of the Ephesians, there is indeed a contrast between their gorgeous splendour and the simplicity of their bread-making. We are informed that their bread was either baked under ashes or upon the hearth. The most usual mode of baking bread was with an earthen or iron pan, broader below than above, in which the loaves were made. These I believe are the lowest types of ovens on record.

The Romans were without doubt far in advance of the Greeks in this matter; as witness the following passage: "To the foreign bakers brought to the City were added a number of freedmen, who were formed into a college, or, as we should say, a corporation. From this corporation the bakers were not allowed to withdraw, and their children were by law under the same obligation; and even those who married the daughters of bakers were obliged to become bakers, or members of the bakers' college." So that it would seem the business of baking was hereditary in Rome. I do not intend to follow up in detail the forms and styles of ovens in vogue among the ancients and in mediæval times, as it would be of little or no practical use, and would merely weary the reader.

The first oven to be mentioned is the common kitchen oven, placed generally at the side of a fireplace, and having, as a rule, from two to four shelves to hold iron plates. It is fitted with a damper, and is heated by the ordinary fire. These ovens are an absolute necessity to the modern housekeeper, and very few houses are built without them. There are many different kinds, but the one I have described is the one in most general use. There is nothing a good housewife values more than a good, serviceable kitchen oven, as it serves for baking all kinds of bread, dinners, pastry, and all manner of tit-bits. Besides, in cold weather it tends to warm the kitchen, and is thus invaluable to a working man's family.

Iron ovens for baking bread on a large scale are fairly common in some places, but are generally found where brick ovens cannot be introduced. I have seen pastry baked to the very pink of perfection in these ovens. But I would recommend a well-set brick oven for loaf bread. Some of the early forms of bakers' ovens are still to be seen in a few country places at the present day. These are built round, with the arch about two feet from the bottom, with no damper save the chimney at the oven mouth. There is no chaffer, or furnace ash-hole, or blow-door. The heating is effected by burning wood in the oven. After the requisite heat has been attained, the fire or ashes are raked out with a large iron rake, and the oven is schuffled or mopped preparatory to the baking.

In one place in Cumberland, where the writer called to see an oven of this kind in operation, the batch was in the oven, the door was closed, and the seams and crevices were stopped up with any matter, objectionable or otherwise, that came to hand, to keep, as a woman said, all the steam in. Some of the bread baked in this oven looked excellent.

WAGGON OVENS.

Waggon ovens may next be mentioned, or pipe and chaffer ovens, as they are called in some districts. These at one time were in extensive use, chiefly in Edinburgh and Liverpool. They are very dirty to work, entailing a great amount of labour; but for baking bread I consider them very good. A large waggon or chaffer is drawn to the oven mouth by the baker, who after ascertaining that the bars are clear, proceeds to start it. Some dry wood, chopped up to certain sizes, must be lit and placed on the waggon bars: when these are burning, well riddled coals are placed on the top. When this is thoroughly set going, he takes a large iron pipe, from twelve to fourteen feet long, according to the size of the oven, and makes it fast by means of a clasp attached to it, to a catch on the waggon, and then runs the waggon to the further end of the oven. The blow-door is then put up and long strips of paper put over the crevices, if there be any, to accelerate the draught. When the baker thinks it has had sufficient blowing there, he moves the waggon from one side to another, and then into the centre, finishing with the oven mouth. During the process of heating the oven, the waggon must be replenished with coal, and great care is needed to prevent any dust from being among it, for should there be dust present the chances are that the oven draught will blow back with a loud report, covering everything in the bakehouse with soot. When the oven has "blown down," as the bakers term it, the waggon occupies a recess in the oven side, built for the purpose. Getting the waggon into its place is the most trying thing in working these ovens. A good strong rake is used to push the waggon into the recess; sometimes this is easily done, but at others the trouble caused is past a joke, and the matter is more serious if there is a quick-going sponge. I once worked a waggon oven, thirteen feet long, for over twelve months; but I shall not care if I never work another.

FURNACE OVENS,

or flush ovens, as they are sometimes called, will next be treated of. They used to be in great repute on account of their easy management. They range from eight to twelve feet long, and the height from the sole of the oven to the crown of the arch varies from two to three feet. The form of this oven is so common that it would be a waste of time to describe it. It is generally heated with coal, and when well built and when the draught is good, I consider it to be a very useful oven. But where the draught is deficient or the coal of inferior quality, there sometimes are what are called cold corners. If such be the case, no full-flavoured, equally baked, showy loaf can be produced, or the heating of the oven got away with as quickly as is necessary.

SCOTCH OVENS,

or Glasgow oven, comes next in order. I will try to describe one. Ten feet long by nine feet wide is the most usually adopted size. The sole of the oven is generally laid with quarrels, or tiles; or, which is a better thing, Ayrshire stone, though this is rather expensive. When the sole is being laid I prefer an almost imperceptible rise to be made from the mouth to the back of the oven—about half an inch in ten feet. The oven walls should be at least one foot thick; eighteen inches would be better if the builder is not restricted with regard to price. The height from the sole to the crown of the arch should be no less than three feet six inches. A groined arch is the best and strongest. A chaffer in the right-hand corner is formed in the shape of a half circle; the flue, ten inches square, is at the left-hand corner, running up, slightly slanting, into the chimney, with a damper at a certain distance with which to blow the oven; the door should be no wider than twenty inches, with a flue above containing a check damper. Round the chaffer should be a fender, six inches in height, to keep in the coke; there is, likewise, a blow-door, through which the ashes fall from the chaffer (for this oven is heated with coke), about fourteen inches wide by ten in height. The heating up can be done in the morning in from an hour and a quarter to an hour and a half. If such an oven as I have described does not give perfect satisfaction, none that I know of will.

Before leaving the subject of Scotch ovens, I will give an idea of what one heating will do. First is baked a batch of 2lb. tins, which generally takes three-quarters of an hour. Then come tea cakes, scones, etc.; after which bun loaves (a tea cake dough with fruit in); next Genoa cake, Madeiras, seed cake, and plum; sometimes other varieties. Then the oven is cooled down with a couple of wet schuffles, to bake 360lbs. of gingerbread. This, at a certain season of the year, is what is daily done with one heating of the oven. It must, however, be kept in mind that these ovens bake solid up to the oven-door.

In Belfast, a place that should be designated "the city of large bakeries," Messrs. Inglis & Co., Limited, have in their bakery a considerable number of Scotch ovens, which enable them to meet the enormous output in that surprising establishment. I may here remark that Messrs. Inglis & Co., and their worthy opponent, Mr. Bernard Hughes, are proprietors of two of the finest bakeries in the world. Both of these firms are a credit to the baking fraternity, and I hope that they are only pioneers to the goal which the baking trade is at no remote period destined to reach.

VARIOUS OTHER OVENS

are now in general use, amongst which may be mentioned the improved travelling chain ovens; improved gas ovens; Perkin's steam ovens; Mason's ovens, which seem to find general favour; the Bailey baker ovens, now in general use in some districts, and various other decker ovens. I have no doubt that all these ovens have some special merit, and will answer the requirements of certain businesses—such for instance as those where 4lb. or 2lb. loaves are baked exclusively.*

There are one, two, and three-decker ovens only recently introduced. I have worked a two-decker oven, but—whether from constant use of one-decker ovens, or from prejudice, I cannot say—I do not like them. An oven, which some large firms have adopted, has been put before the public having travelling withdrawable baking plates running on casters, so that the whole bottom of the oven can be filled by hand and run into the oven at the same moment, and drawn out when baked. But from what I learn—only by hearsay—I think they are not much in favour among bakers.

The Climax withdrawable oven is one of the latest constructions in oven building; but I have not seen this new invention in working operation, and therefore do not feel justified in commenting on it.

But I must say that, in my opinion, the oven has yet to be built that can beat the Scotch oven, especially for a mixed trade.

---

*When employers are putting down new decker ovens, the convenience of the workman seems to be seldom thought of. The baking capacity of these ovens and the small space occupied by them seem to be the principal points aimed at; the great amount of inconvenience and the excessive heat which in most cases the journeyman is subjected to are altogether ignored.

In the working of these ovens no poking or raking is required, nor is there the chance of filling the bakehouse half-full of stifling smoke, which is too often the case in the working of the old style of oven. All that is required is to feed your oven with a certain quantity of coke, keeping your eye on the pyrometer if you have one attached to the oven, and shutting or closing your damper to maintain an even heat of say 520°. If this method be followed hot and cold ovens will be avoided. The accuracy of my remarks may be proved by testing them in practice.

GENERAL DETAILS.

THE VENTILATION OF BAKEHOUSES.

Fresh air is as necessary to life and health as is wholesome food. At every breath our lungs deprive the air of oxygen, and we breathe out a large quantity of carbonic acid. Now carbonic acid acts as a poison, and discharged breath is, therefore, more or less poisoned air, so that if, instead of inhaling fresh air, we take into the lungs air that has been already breathed, the blood is deprived of the oxygen necessary to enable it to warm and support the body. Therefore through ineffective ventilation, or, which is worse, no ventilation at all, we run the risk of poisoning the blood, and causing disease—the forerunner of death. Physicians declare that such diseases as consumption and scrofula are due far more to poisoned air, inhaled in our houses and factories, than to cold or a changeable climate. If any baker leaves an imperfectly ventilated bakehouse and goes into the fresh air for five minutes, he will, on returning, if gifted with an average amount of intelligence, be shocked at the atmosphere in which he has been living for hours. If the danger mentioned above exists in ordinary houses and workshops, it is not pleasant to think of the condition of dark, underground, badly lighted, and as badly ventilated bakehouses. Like a plant deprived of light, white and stunted in stalk and leaves, so is our poor journeyman baker of pallid, woebegone countenance, because compelled to earn a livelihood in what are little better than fever dens! To work well one must feel well, but under such unfavourable conditions the majority of bakers are unable to do so. Our legislators are to a certain extent to blame for the existence of such a state of things.

THE EFFECT OF COLD OR CHILLED DOUGH ON THE HEAT OF AN OVEN.

In large and draughty bakehouses where no heating apparatus is attached, the air of the workshop in cold weather is liable to have a chilling effect on the dough; it likewise has a corresponding effect on the ovens, and must in consequence cool the oven sooner. It is advisable in such bakehouses to have the heat of the ovens a few degrees higher than if they were to be filled with dough not so chilled. To make my meaning clearer, suppose a baker were to run a batch of bread into an oven of, say, 500° F., with the dough at a temperature of 66° F., and then put another batch into another oven of the same heat, with the dough at a temperature of 76° F., the bloom, texture, and flavour of these respective batches could not possibly be the same. A practical man will at once see that this variation in the heat of the dough must, in the natural order of cause and effect, be met by an alteration in the heat of the oven to suit it, so as in some measure, as in the case we have supposed, to equalise their different temperatures. But happily this little wrinkle is very seldom required in a well-appointed modern bakery.

HEATING NEW OVENS.

When starting to heat a new oven the manager of the bakehouse should see that the sole is covered with sawdust, and that the oven is blown up to a gentle heat. Too much heat at first is liable to make the sole expand and the tiles crack, and cause other damage. The sawdust will partly protect the sole till it is a little seasoned. The chaffer should be well filled at night, and the door left open half an inch to allow of the exit of the fuel gas. If the door were shut the gas would put out the fire. Four to six days are required to heat a brick oven.

SEASONING BREAD TINS.

All new bread tins ought to be properly seasoned before being used. They require to be put in an oven of an ordinary heat for about one hour. If treated in this manner the tins wear longer, and a better crust can be got on the loaves when baked. When the tins are properly seasoned, the bread they contain requires less time to bake.

HOW TO USE UP OLD BREAD.

When a baker finds he has a surplus stock of old bread on hand, the most profitable method of using it up is to make it into bread raspings. It is readily sold at fourpence per pound, to use with fish, hams, soups, and other dainties in the kitchen. The mode of procedure is as follows: Cut the bread into pieces an inch square, and place them into the oven to be well dried. They must be as dry as rusks. When dry, place a quantity on the table and bruise them with a 4lb. weight. With a large rolling or paste pin crush the bruised parts till the whole is of the consistency of fine sand, when it is put away in barrels or boxes for use; or they may be lightly crushed and then ground through a coffee-mill. Sour bread is of no use for raspings on account of its flavour.

HOW TO ASCERTAIN THE HEAT OF WATER.

Hold a thermometer in the water and keep moving it gently about for twenty-four seconds; it will then register the exact temperature. This system is more practical than the old style of taking the heat of the water by dipping the hand in it, as by it the baker can work his sponges to a safer and truer degree of exactitude.

A STANDARD FOR BREAD.

This would be a novel thing for bakers to adopt. But, as I have said in preceding chapters, progress is the order of the day, and as it is a growing want something of the sort will be adopted. I am not aware that at bread exhibitions there is any particular standard in force for judging the respective merits of bread sent in for competition, general appearance alone being considered. If this is the case it is high time there was something more conclusive, as although a loaf's appearance ought to go a long way in its favour, it is not everything, for the taste should also be taken into consideration. I would suggest the adoption of a standard in which the loaf's merits were considered in something after this order : flavour, texture, colour, moisture, shape, etc. A test like this would stimulate the trade, and help to rouse it from that somewhat happy-go-lucky state into which it has fallen. There are surely men capable enough to assist in the proper consideration of the subject, and to agitate ably enough to secure a successful and creditable issue.

ON CARRYING FLOUR.

The time has arrived when this question ought to be settled once and for all. A journeymen baker is neither a Samson nor a Hercules (although I have seen members of our craft who could hold their own in many a well-contested battle); but apart from that, to expect a baker, who perhaps has been at work when other tradesmen have been sleeping, to carry thirty, forty, or it may be fifty sacks of flour, each weighing 280lbs., is a stigma on the civilising elements of the nineteenth century. All flours should be put up in sacks of 140lbs., that is, in 10st. sacks. Journeymen bakers ought themselves to make a move in this matter. It is for those who will follow us, as well as for those now engaged in the trade, that I make this appeal. Future generations of bakers must think that those of the present day were a simple, cowardly lot to have borne the yoke so long. I speak from experience, for I am sorry to say I have seen men carry flour till their shoulders were running with blood. Think of that, ye trade regenerators! Yet this pernicious system is still carried on, more from want of thought than for any pecuniary advantage derived by the millers. However, I see a move has been made in the direction of compelling millers to adopt the ten-stone system. One and all should do their utmost to stop this barbarous practice.

MACHINERY, TOOLS, ETC.

This is an age of progress, and I think if machinery had not come to the aid of the baker the trade would have been in a sorry plight in this country.

That facilities are wanted now more than in the time of our forefathers the present position of the trade will testify; and my hope is that bakers may meet in a kindly, receptive spirit the various inventions in machinery that are yearly being introduced for their benefit. That great changes of an almost revolutionary character have taken place none will deny. Old systems have been superseded, old plans entirely disregarded, and novel ways and ideas are daily coming into vogue. By contrasting old modes and customs for the making of bread with the modern systems, it will readily be seen that great progress has been made. The old-fashioned method, with the drudgery of its sponging, doughing, and oven work is rapidly passing away, and a method more healthy, cleanly, and expeditious is taking its place. A modern bakery has plenty of room and light, and a thorough system of sanitary arrangements. It has an oven heat indicator, a flour-testing apparatus, and bread machinery.

The first thing I will touch upon in machinery is the dough-kneading machine, which is one of the greatest boons a baker can have; together with a gas engine. The amount of work performed by a dough-kneader is almost incredible. Before passing from the doughing machine, I would just remark that an inefficient man at the mixer or kneader will go a long way towards spoiling the dough by keeping it too long in the mixer—a thing tending to kill the dough and seriously injure the gluten, which makes the bread dry and flinty.

There is also the dough-dividing machine. I have never worked this, but if it has any of the merits possessed by the bun divider, it cannot fail to be another boon to the trade.

From practical experience I may say that there has not yet been found a proper substitute in the shape of a dough mixer than can compete with hand-made dough; and any bread made by a doughing machine that I have seen comes short in feel and texture to bread made by hand.

Again, there is the flour-sifting machine, which greatly assists in the cleanliness of bread; also the sponge-whisking machine. In the old style of sponge-beating one might be pardoned a muttered malediction on the inventor of sponges when one could scarcely give the whisk another turn. The creaming machine is good in its way, and the peel cutter has prevented many a blistered hand. The currant and sultana washer and drier is another requisite. Thus the old system of making bread is vanishing, deposed by newer and better modes.

PYROMETERS.

I would advise any baker intending to build new ovens to get one of these heat indicators, as I find them very convenient in registering the oven's heat. Where they are used the baker has not to work in a haphazard way. But where it is inconvenient to get one, I should advise the baker to procure a special size square edged tin to hold his coal or coke, and he will soon get to know exactly how much coal or coke is required to obtain the proper heat. Different ovens, flours, and modes of sponging require different heats, but the average is about 500°.

UTENSILS REQUIRED FOR A MODERN BAKERY.

It is necessary for a bakery to be supplied with all the latest improvements for producing bread with speed and of good quality.

It is worse than foolish for a small firm with only the primitive style of utensils to try to compete with large bakeries. In some cases a man of the old school may, I will not say succeed, but hold his own, by long hours and hard fighting, but no one can prosper without modern plant.

There are some men so prejudiced and narrow-minded in any matters of improvement that they would run the chance of liquidation and the gauntlet of the Bankruptcy Court rather than be suspected of using any novel apparatus, or introducing it into their bakehouses; who will also plainly tell you that what was good enough for their forefathers may serve for them. These men are a drag on civilisation's wheel; they cannot see a week in advance of them; they have no noble instincts to break the bounds of their narrow-minded sphere; men—unworthy of the name—who would consider it a crime to remove the difficulties or soften the sorrows and troubles of their fellow-men. I believe that the introduction of modern education, machinery, and tools, with the healthy information given by our trade journals, will make our craft in the near future second to none. But let me advise the trade journals to try to bury the hatchet of controversy and allow the stream of peace and harmony to run free; then shall we look upon them as the guiding stars of the trade.

Let us then be of one accord in welcoming any useful improvement, noble idea, or better suggestion. We must try to leave the trade in a better condition than we found it, by working for brother tradesmen as well as for ourselves, and instructing and helping one another in order to give it that impetus it so much needs. When chemistry is introduced into our Board schools, and made one of the elements of ordinary education, we shall see with what systematic exactness the manufacture of bread can be conducted.

Of all the requirements of a bakery I think good ovens are the most important. Flour, yeast, tools, in fact nearly everything else can be changed ; but when once the ovens are built they remain, as a rule, stationary. So a baker should see that his ovens are the very best that can be built, for on them depend, in a great measure, his chances of success. An oven ten feet long and nine feet broad is quite large enough for successful working, with a pyrometer or heat indicator. Next is the engine, if the bakery is of any size. A gas engine about $2\frac{1}{2}$ horse-power will save a great amount of manual labour. It is likewise more expeditious if there is a trade of anything like fifty or a hundred sacks per week. The gas engine is easily managed, and can be put in motion at a moment's notice. There should always be plenty of hot water at hand ; but I do not approve of boilers on the top of chaffers in the oven. Separate boilers are the rule with large firms ; so that if barm is used, the water to make it can be had from them. There should also be a cistern for hot and cold water, with a thermometer and a gauge attached. This latter is a handy little article. A doughing or mixing machine, of the most approved pattern, is also wanted. Troughs —or " trows," as the baker calls them—should be made of clean dry wood, of a handy size, with casters, so that they can be run under the cistern. A good set of barm or quarter tubs is required ; and if there is not an office, a writing desk would not be amiss for the convenience of manager or foreman. Then there are the setters, or " upsets," where batch bread is made, for keeping the loaves from the oven side, etc. They are placed at the sides, back, and front, and are generally of beech, five inches in height and an inch and a half thick. In large firms, a large proving press, of wood, is used in which to put the loaves to prove. It has two doors, and a glass panel to enable the workmen to see within, and is generally heated with a perforated gas-pipe bent square or oval. A cistern, lined with zinc, is placed over the gas and partly filled with water, and the press is heated by the steam rising therefrom. A tap is attached to the pipe to control the gas.

A small set of drawers, twelve in number, like a chest, will be found very handy. Each drawer should be made so that it will go in the oven, to be used for proving rolls, baps, scones, etc. Large boards are needed for placing loaves upon when they are rolled up or moulded. Sometimes these are made to fit into the table on slides. Carrying boards are also wanted to put the bread on when drawn from the oven. In large bakeries trucks are used to convey bread to the bread-room. A hand truck is useful for moving sacks of flour. There should be likewise a long rod, or schuffle, with an iron swivel and a ring at the end, to which is attached a piece of net or sacking to clean out the oven. Three or four peels are generally required for each oven—a running peel, very light, with a light mahogany mouth screwed on at the rod end; a drawing peel, heavier and stronger, for drawing out the bread; one for drawing pan bread; and a general peel. The three latter should be made from well-seasoned English elm. A schuffle tub is another thing wanted, also one or two wire sieves, besides a patent flour sifter. Then loaf pans to hold half-quarters, three half-quarters, four half-quarters, two quarters, and three quarters. These sizes are used mostly in Scotland. One-loaf pans are greatly used in England for 4lb. and 2lb. loaves. Flat tins, usually edged all round, about thirty inches long and eighteen broad, are also required; besides sandwich, diet, milk, and Coburg tins; two or three pairs of bakehouse scales; a large flour-weighing machine; barm sieves, butter brushes, wash brushes, table brushes; loaf bread cases; bread stabbers or dockers; weights; a set of oven-bricks for keeping the setters up in front of the batch; a set of water or barm tins ; pint, quart, half-gallon and gallon tins ; scrapers, or "scarts," as they are called in Scotland ; and a set of good tables to work the bread dough upon. I have seen tables placed in the centre of the bakehouse—the handiest part of the shop—with a quarter-inch iron edging to keep the dough on and the flour from falling off. Two or three large flour scoops are required to feed the doughing-machine ; also one or two small scoops ; "clicks," to rake the "clinkers" off the chaffer ; a pedal to feed the chaffer ; and a thermometer—not forgetting large sponging tubs for setting quick sponges ; dough knives, about the size of a large carver ; sprint boards, floor brushes, etc. A good bakery is also fitted up with a lavatory.

Amongst the latest improvements for a modern bakery is a steam generator for supplying ovens with steam. The contrivance in question is patented by Mr. Thoms, and is very highly spoken of ; but I am under the impression that a batch of bread, properly manipulated and baked in an oven that is built on the best principles, should generate sufficient steam of itself to satisfy the most critical and fastidious of bakers. The new patent light for ovens should likewise take its place as a sound improvement in helping the ovenman to fill and draw ovens.

ADULTERATION.

ALUM, POTATOES, ETC.

I am indebted to Reid's Guide to the trade for the following. This work is now scarce, being out of print, but in its time it must have been a useful *multum in parvo* to the baking trade.

"Alum and potatoes are now considered indispensable by the London bakers in the manufacture of seconds or household bread, *i.e.*, the bread in daily use in the metropolis. The effect of alum upon bread is not well understood, but it is generally supposed to bleach and act as an astringent. Accum says that the theory of the bleaching properties of alum, as manifested in the panification (making into bread) of an inferior kind of flour, is by no means well understood; and indeed it is really surprising that the effect should be produced by so small a quantity of that substance; two or three ounces of alum being sufficient for a sack of flour."

From experiments in which Mr. Reid had been employed, with the assistance of skilful bakers, he was authorised to state that without the addition of alum it does not appear possible to make white, light, and porous bread, such as is used in the metropolis, unless the flour be of the very best quality. Such an assertion as the above, if made to a modern baker who has studied the why and wherefore of fermentation, would be ridiculed.

Mr. Reid continues to say :—

"Mr. A. Booth, the lecturer on chemistry, asserts that alum bleaches from the attraction of alumina, one of its constituents, to the colouring matter of the flour, and also acts as an astringent to the bread.

"If these opinions are to be relied upon, of course the question is settled as to the indispensability of alum in making London bread. Accum asserts that he, in conjunction with skilful bakers, has tested the thing by experiments which prove that alum cannot be dispensed with. For my part I am inclined to believe that the whiteness of the London bread is due in some degree to the process of baking—a process widely differing from that followed by women who make home-made bread, which, as I have before asserted, is never so white or so porous as baker's bread, though made of the same flour.

"Accum, whatever talent he might possess as a chemist, was a fraudulent writer; and, therefore, his assertions are not to be relied upon. As to the experiments which he alleges he made, I agree with him, however, in his observation that the theory of the bleaching properties of alum, etc., is by no means well understood!"

If, as Accum asserts, he had tested the properties of alum in bread, his testing "apparatus" and "skilful bakers" must have been of a very low order to allow of such a grave assertion. I have myself tested the properties of alum in bread with modern appliances, and have found the very reverse of what Accum wishes us to believe.

Mr. Reid again says:

"The quantity of alum used in baking is much less than the public generally imagine, even by the most fraudulent of cheap-bread bakers; and indeed much less than many of the bakers themselves imagine. This may appear a strange assertion; and it is probably one never made before in print; but a little explanation will make the point quite clear. It is well known that the bakers are liable to a heavy fine if alum is found on their premises. To avoid the liability as much as possible they have been in the habit of buying their alum ready powdered at the druggist's, under the name of 'stuff.'

"The druggists keep the 'stuff,' which the bakers imagine is unadulterated ground or powdered alum, but which is in reality a compound, consisting of one part of alum to three parts of muriate of soda, i.e., common table salt. This compound is made by pounding the salt with the alum in the mortar. It is kept at the druggist's in pound packages, sold at twopence each.

"For this statement I have the authority of several druggists, and the evidence of my own eyes. Extraordinary as it may seem that bakers should allow themselves to be so cheated, I nevertheless believe it to be a fact. It should be recollected that few bakers are readers, and rarely of scientific or medical works.

"In the fourth edition of Gray's 'Supplement to the Pharmacopœia and Treatise on Pharmacology,' under the head of 'Stuff,' this term is thus defined:

"'Alum, in small crystals, 1lb., common salt, 3lbs., to mix with flour for baking.'

"I have the evidence of my own senses for the knowledge that respectable bakers of home or household bread do not put more than eight ounces of stuff to a bag of flour; and this 'stuff,' on Gray's authority, contains only a quarter, or two ounces, of alum, the remainder being common salt. Some persons, however, ask for powdered alum; but the druggist, knowing from the quantity required and his customer's appearance that it is wanted for baking purposes, invariably serves him with the afore-mentioned mixture of salt and alum. This I have frequently seen done. The druggist's object is profit. It would scarcely be worth his while to sell powdered alum at twopence a pound. Gray puts it at 1s. 6d. a pound. This is ridiculously high to sell by the pound, but it is generally sold at a penny an ounce. When the writer gave this information to his baker he exclaimed, 'You don't say so! The infamous rogues! Why, the rascally druggists cheat us before we can cheat our customers!'

"Such being the case, it seems almost inconceivable that so small a quantity as two ounces of alum in 280lbs. of flour—the weight of a sack—should have any effect in bleaching, especially when we consider that one hundred parts of alum contain but a fraction over ten parts of alumina, the only constituent in alum, I am informed, that possesses bleaching powers and properties.

Nevertheless, there can be no doubt that alum—perhaps not singly, but in conjunction with other ingredients—has the effect of whitening the bread.

"A circumstance occurred—I have this on indisputable authority—in the experience of a baker, who by accident left out of his dough the usual quantity of stuff, containing no more than 2oz. of alum. The consequence was a batch of brown bread, necessarily sold at half price."

> "There are more things in heaven and earth, Horatio,
> than are dreamt of in your philosophy."—*Hamlet.*

I have now given the reader Mr. Reid's opinion of alum in bread. What his motive could have been in trying to underrate the bad effects of alum I do not know, as Mr. Reid was too much of a theoretical tradesman not to have thought differently from what he wrote. But this written opinion will serve another purpose—it shows that at the time of writing the above, adulterating bread with alum was a recognised custom, and much more extensively adopted than he professes.

Herr Van Hamel Ross has recently at Amsterdam detected 30 per cent. of marble dust in ground rice imported from Paris. In Haute Vienne one of the most extensive millers of the district has been found to mix carbonate of lead with his flour. This fraud gives the flour a fine appearance, renders it whiter, and enables the dealer to pass off inferior qualities at the price of a better article. The customer is liable, among other misfortunes, to lead poisoning—a trifling consideration to the flourishing, fraudulent manufacturer. Dr. Darwin says that when much alum is used it may be distinguished by the eye in the place where two loaves have stuck together in the oven—they break from each other with a much smoother surface than where alum does not exist. I do not recognise this test, having seen batch bread, when drawn from the oven, with a smoothness and texture unsurpassed by any alum-adulterated bread, however skilful in the use of alum a baker may be. The bread referred to was set or sponged with a flying or quick sponge, containing nothing but pure flour, water, yeast, and salt. According to Pownall's work on the "Assize of Bread," bakers were their own flour manufacturers, and were required by the statutes of assize to manufacture a certain quantity and to sell the bread at a fixed price. But the assize of bread has for a long time been abolished, and the baker now sells his bread for as much as anyone is willing to pay for it. But there is still a heavy penalty demanded from a baker retailing bread short of weight. Potatoes, called by bakers "fruit," were used at one time for assisting fermentation, and were said to give flavour, and improve the appearance of bread. I do not hold these qualities to be very essential to a baker's success, and he must be very unskilful who cannot produce the qualities desired without resorting to potatoes.

Let us see what the great scientist Liebig says on the subject.

"To make bread cheaper it has been proposed to add to dough potato starch or dextrine, rice, the pressed pulp of turnips, pressed raw potatoes, etc. But all these additions only diminish the nutritive value of bread. Potato starch, dextrine, or the pressed pulp of turnips and beet-root, when added to flour yield a mixture the nutritive value of which is equal to the entire potato, or lower still. But no one can consider the change of grain or flour into a food of equal value with potatoes, or rice, an improvement. The true problem is to render the potatoes or rice similar or equal to wheat in their effects, and not *vice-versa*. It is better under all circumstances to boil the potatoes and eat them as such, than to add potatoes or potato-starch to flour before it is made into bread. This should be strictly prohibited by police regulation, on account of the cheating to which it would inevitably give rise."

Potatoes, however, as well as damaged rice, have been, and no doubt are now used by cheap fraudulent bakers; but I emphatically deny the stories I have heard about bakers using *ground bones* to adulterate bread; and for this reason—the expense of making them fit for such a purpose would be greater than the cost of the flour itself. There are instances on record of bakers being convicted for using gypsum, chalk, and pipe-clay.

Mr. Davy, Professor of Chemistry, says that carbonate of magnesia, used in the proportion of twenty to forty grains to one pound of flour, materially improves bread. But, from personal experience, I very much doubt whether any of the obnoxious ingredients mentioned help in any way to improve the appearance or the flavour of a loaf of bread. I must in all fairness say that, so far as I can learn, there never has been a time in the history of the baking trade when the consumer has been better protected, or a better class of bread has been put before the public, than the present. We may in a great measure thank the Food Adulteration Act for this; but I only give the baker his due in expressing the belief that education, with its civilising effect, has more to do with the present state of affairs than laws passed in order to keep him in the path of honesty.

A baker occupies a post of more responsibility than the generality of the public give him credit for. For instance, when a person fed on bread of a sour, heavy, sodden, unpalatable nature is compared with one in the same condition of life, fed on good, light, porous bread, of a fine nutty flavour, common sense will indicate which of them enjoys life best, or thinks it best worth living, when the chances of taking an active part in life, and of building up a strong, robust constitution, are so unequal. I think, therefore, the public ought to be a little more compassionate to the poor journeyman baker, whose lot is by no means one of the pleasantest in the world.

APPENDIX.

BAKING AND BAKERS IN THE TIME OF THE ROMANS.

Associated as bakers are with a necessary article of food in daily use, of which we are never satiated, as in the case of other food, bread itself is surrounded with a wealth of history; from its origin, so crude, to the varieties of later times; concerning the forms in which it was made; the reverence in which it was held; the abundance, and the want of it, with the substitutes used to satisfy the craving for it, or made use of by less civilised people in days gone past. I will in the first place try to show bakers what their position has been, especially in the time of the Romans.

In 1834 the Society for the Diffusion of Useful Knowledge published two volumes of a work entitled "Pompeii." This work is of great interest to the baker, as it lifts the veil from the hidden past and reveals to him what, but for the destruction of Pompeii, would never have been known, *viz.*, some of the customs and usages of the baking trade 1800 years ago. Until I read this work I had no idea that the baker was provided with a goddess, Fornax, the goddess of the oven. It goes on to say that the Romans were very careless of the amount of labour wasted in preparing an article of daily and universal consumption. This probably arose chiefly from the employment of slaves, the hardness of whose tasks none cared about; while the profit and encouragement to enterprise on the part of the baker was proportionately diminished, since every wealthy family prepared its bread at home.

But the same inattention to the useful arts pervaded all they did. Their skill in working metals was equal to ours. Nothing can be more beautiful than the execution of tripods, lamps, and vases; nothing coarser than their locks—at the same time the door handles, bolts, etc., which were placed where they would be seen, were often exquisitely wrought. But the demands of a luxurious nobility would never have repaid any man for devoting his attention to the improvement of mills—(I here refer to the hand mills the Roman bakers had for grinding their corn)—and there was little general commerce to set their ingenuity to work.

Originally, mills were turned by hand, and this severe labour seems, in all half-savage times, to have been conducted by women. It was so in Egypt (see Exod. xi. 5); it was so in Greece in the time of Homer, who employed fifty females in the house of Alcinous upon this service; it was so in Palestine in the time of the Evangelists; and in England in the 14th and 16th centuries. Harrison, the historian, two centuries later, says that his wife ground her malt at home upon her quern. Those who had been guilty of an offence were sent to the mill as a punishment, and sometimes forced to work in chains.

The oven of the Roman baker was made with considerable attention to economy of heat. The real oven was enclosed in a sort of ante-oven, the latter having an aperture in the top for the smoke to escape, and a hole in the side for the introduction of dough, which was prepared in an adjoining room, and deposited through that hole on a shovel. The bread when baked was placed in a room on the other side of the oven, through a similar aperture, to cool. For a long time bakers used their corn sodden into pap; and there were no bakers in Rome before the war against Pyrrhus, King of Macedonia (Pliny, xviii.) about A.U. 580. Before this, every house made its own bread, and even after the invention of bread, it was long before mills were known. Their loaves appear to have been very often baked in moulds, several of which have been found. They may possibly be *artopae*, and the loaves *artopicii*. Several of these loaves have been discovered; they are flat, and about eight inches in diameter. One in the Neapolitan has a stamp on the top.

Thus we have here a description of both ovens and bread, 1800 years ago. If Britain be destined to relapse into such a state of barbarism as Italy passed through in the period which divides ancient and modern history, its inhabitants a thousand years hence will know, we hope, a little more of the manual process of bread-baking in our time, than we do of the ancient Roman baking trade.

Three bakers' shops have been discovered in a tolerable state of preservation in Pompeii; the mills, the oven, kneading troughs, vessels for containing water, as well as flour and leaven being also found. One of these shops was attached to the house of Sallust; another to the house of Pansa, and these were no doubt worth a very handsome rent to the proprietors.

In every Roman bakehouse there was a chief, or master, called *patronus*. This person had the superintendence of the bakehouse and the ordering of all matters therein. These patrons elected every year one out of their number who had the care of the college and the scrutiny of the general body. That bakers were highly respected by the Romans is proved by the fact that, although as individuals they could own no property, yet now and then one became a senator. And indeed in every nation the first bakers were highly respected. Whether this arose from the eating of good fermented bread instead of hard unleavened cake, it is hard to determine. Pharoah's chief baker, it is plain, was regarded by his master as one of the most important men in Egypt, from the fact that he was consulted upon a matter affecting the personal comfort of the monarch.

By the statutes of England bakers are considered superior to those employed in handicrafts. "No man"—according to 22nd Henry VIII., cap. 13—" for using the mysteries of the science of baking, brewing, surveying, or writing shall be interpreted a handicraftsman." Thus it appears that bakers, like writers—now called attorneys—are gentlemen by Act of Parliament; but it is a remarkable fact that no baker has ever risen to the honour of the Lord Mayoralty of the City of London.

However, to return to the Romans. The ancient bakers had hand-mills near their ovens; these were originally nothing more than pestles and mortars with which they reduced corn to flour. Let the reader pause for a moment, if he be a baker, and contrast this slow system of grinding with the expensive and elaborate machinery now in use. What a great change from the customs of the misty past! The bakers were called in Latin (as were the millers previous to the introduction of baking as a profession), *pistores*, or pounders. For the same reason the Roman bake-houses were called *pistoria*. The Roman college or incorporation of bakers had granted to them all the mill utensils, slaves, animals, and everything, in short, that belonged to the *pistoria*. In addition to these the corporation received considerable land, and nothing was withheld that could assist them in pursuing their trade or profession to the best advantage. It appears that the more laborious part of the business, such as grinding the corn, etc., was not performed by the bakers themselves, as persons found guilty of petty offences were condemned to work for a certain period in the bakehouses, and even the judges of Africa were obliged every five years to send to Rome such criminals as had incurred that kind of punishment. The bakehouses, of which in the time of Augustus there were no less than 329, were distributed over the fourteen divisions of the city, and no baker could pass from one bakehouse to another without special permission; they were not permitted to attend gladiatorial shows, much less to become gladiators themselves, nor to be connected with the comedians. To the care of the Roman bakers the public granaries were committed; they paid nothing for the corn used in baking bread that was to be given to the poor citizens, and the price of that intended to be sold was regulated by the magistrates. No corn was given out of these granaries except for the use of the bakehouses or for that of the emperor, and it is recorded that if any baker were convicted of having converted any part of the grain belonging to the public granaries to his own or any improper use, he was made to pay a fine of 500lbs. of gold—so enormous a sum of money that we cannot help doubting the truth of the statement. It is also recorded that when the Gauls sought to subjugate Rome, the god Jupiter suggested a novel mode of defending the city—namely, pounding their assailants with loaves of bread! and I believe that they were so well pounded with such a host of these strange weapons that the besiegers, who had relied on starving out the Romans, shortly withdrew. We are told that the younger Gracchus, for the sake of popularity, compelled the state to sell corn at a loss to all Roman citizens.

Our Saxon ancestors knew but little about bread. In the days of Queen Elizabeth the bread at meal times was handed round on the point of a sharp knife. It is but a short step from good Queen Bess to James I. The art of cookery, instead of advancing, must have fallen to a low ebb in this reign, as I believe the feasting was of barbarous kind, and the dishes prepared were of a questionable nature. In 1661, at a feast, four huge pigs were served, harnessed and bitted, with strings of sausages attached to a monstrous bag pudding. Snails, frogs, and curiosities dished up and made palatable were the fit accompaniments of the riotous feasting that set in, the expenses of which for one year in the Royal household amounted to the respectable figure of £100,000; not a bad sum in those times for the treasury to meet. It is also recorded that Charles II. was very fond of specially prepared gingerbread, but my opinion is that this king and his court, according to history, required something more substantial than common gingerbread to satiate their discriminating appetites.

From the time of King Charles to that of Queen Victoria, nothing occurred to elevate or develop our trade, which, still harassed with old superstitions and customs, struggled in mists it could not dispel till the year 1845—June 26th, when the Repeal of the Corn Laws was secured. Then the baking trade commenced to draw itself together; a few inquiring minds came to the front; and the baking trade awoke to new life. From that time to the present what stupendous improvements have been made in the plant of a bakery! Sponging is still left to us as an incubus, and seems to baffle the most learned, scientific, and foremost men of our time; but that a barm, or yeast, will by and by be produced to meet the requirements of the age I do not for a moment doubt. When yeast, or barm, was first used for the purpose of raising dough I have no reliable information; it seems hidden in past ages.

THE FOREIGN ELEMENT IN LONDON

is one of the principal causes of the degraded state of many London bakers. What excuse is to be found for the competition to which a British-born baker is subjected, I fail to see. If the foreigner were to compete on equal terms with the British baker, there would be little cause for fear ; but it is not so, for they come over in droves and glut the market, working for wages scarcely exceeding those of our lads, and for hours that are by their length a disgrace to humanity. A practical Englishman has either to compete with this scum—I will not disgrace the trade by calling them men—or take the consequences. I should propose to agitate for a tax on foreign bakers, and take a leaf out of Australia's book, as that country now does respecting the Chinese, for I am sure the public will never interfere so long as they can get cheap bread. If any other country were subjected to such hard laws as the bakers are in this, means would soon be found for the subjects' protection. Free America protects her institutions against paupers being landed; here they can come in shoals and no questions are asked. Freedom is one of man's greatest blessings ; but freedom at another's expense is not true freedom. Away with cant ! Let the bakers be protected ; the public would also be benefited.

The bakers of London constitue the 19th company. They were incorporated about the year 1307, and have a master, four wardens, thirty assistants, and liverymen and commonalty.

JOURNEYMAN BAKERS IN LONDON.

" All things have rest ; why should we toil alone ?
We only toil who are the first of things,
And make perpetual moan.
Still from one labour to another thrown,
Nor even fold our wings
Nor cease from wanderings."—*Tennyson.*

The journeyman baker begins work at eleven o'clock at night, and after a night's work of a most laborious nature, he starts with the ferment. At six in the morning he mixes his ferment, and re-heats the oven a little for the rolls, cottage bread, etc., which are made from part of the common bread dough set aside for the purpose, its superior lightness being due to a longer proving. While the rolls and cottage loaves are baking, he carries the bread just baked into the shop, and then cleans out the bakehouse—that is, he washes the seasoning tubs, scrapes out the troughs, and cleans up generally. The rolls by this time are about ready to draw from the oven and be sent to the shop. He next takes his breakfast in the bakehouse, and when all is done and everything ready the bakings for the public begin to come in. This will occupy him till about one o'clock; the poor man now gets his dinner; from two till four he is out serving customers; about five he sets his sponge, and then washes down his hand van. It is now well on for six o'clock, when he is supposed to go to bed and sleep till eleven, at which time his sponge will be ready. After he has made the dough and set away the ovens, he will have an hour's sleep. By this time his dough is ready to throw out upon the table; he then weighs off, moulds, and sets the batch, as it is called in London. Now he may have another sleep, and then comes the drawing of the batch, etc. This is considered an easy place! and a man has to have a good character to get it. On Saturday night I have seen men at work up to ten o'clock, and then have to be in the bakehouse early on Sunday morning, to prepare the ovens for Sunday's baking. All this, too, is done in an unhealthy atmosphere in a confined cellar. This is known as a single-handed place; the man is called a Scotch foreman. There are better places than this in London, but they are the exception. This system is carried on daily in the most civilised city in the world, and the wages paid for such slavery are from £1 to 26s. per week—surely not sufficient to keep a man honest. Were the London bakers better paid, and had they to work more Christianlike hours, we should hear less about London bakers being convicted for making "dead uns," or "dead men"—charging a credit customer for six loaves, for instance, when they only deliver four. Some of my readers may think that I am overpainting this horrid state of things. But let me mention as a fact that it has been officially stated, as recently as the month of January, 1891, at a coroner's inquest held in the east end of London, on the body of a baker's child who literally died from starvation, that the father of the child was working seventeen and eighteen hours per day for the mere pittance of three shillings and sixpence per week. What has come over Britain's boasted Christianity and philanthropy when we find ourselves among facts like these? Well may bakers quote Burns's poem, "Man was made to mourn." One verse is very appropriate in their case:

> "Oh, Death! the poor man's dearest friend—
> The kindest and the best!
> Welcome the hour my aged limbs
> Are laid with thee at rest!
> The great, the wealthy, fear thy blow,
> From pomp and pleasure torn!
> But oh! a blest relief to those
> That weary-laden mourn!"

JOURNEYMAN BAKERS IN GLASGOW.

> "In the world's broad field of battle,
> In the bivouac of Life,
> Be not like dumb, driven cattle!
> Be a hero in the strife!"

The condition of the journeyman baker in Glasgow is somewhat similar to that of his London brother; and it is surprising to see how they have fallen into such a low, depressed state, when we consider the high condition they held as a body of tradesmen only twelve or fifteen years ago. At that time Glasgow was looked up to as a model of excellence—so much so, that all the provincial towns in Scotland used to vie with each other in trying to imitate her. Now a cruel magician's wand has been waved over the place, and all is changed: the smallest town in Scotland can show a cleaner sheet; or in other words, the provincial bakers as a body, both as regards hours of labour, and wages, are a long way in advance of those in Glasgow—with the exception, of course, of the middlemen or managers. And this has come about, I think, through the amount of competition for work that exists to drag men into the mire. The factory system is carried on in Glasgow to a far greater extent than in any other town in Great Britain; and as most factories distribute their bread in vans through the different districts, those men who can get their bread into the market first, have the best chance of disposing of it. One factory started to get their bread out an hour before another; here is where the thin edge of the wedge was inserted. I can assure my readers that the whole of the wedge is in now with a vengeance, and employers and middlemen would not hesitate to drive another wedge in if it could be managed. At one time the baker's work in Glasgow for one day was to produce 34 dozen 2lb. loaves for one man; that was considered a fair day's work, and on a par with the hardest of any other tradesmen; but now it is not an exceptional case for a baker to have to produce 40 dozen loaves per man a day. And that man lives in a Christian community, and in the nineteenth century. O ye gods! think of it! Well might our bard say "Man's inhumanity to man makes countless thousands mourn!"

But there is now an association formed in Scotland, and formed, I think, on a firm basis, that will in time, let us hope, place Glasgow bakers in their once proud position; and I would advise the journeymen bakers of that venerable city to take Longfellow's advice, and

> "Be not like dumb, driven cattle!
> Be a hero in the strife!"

Now a word to the employers. I would ask them, is not the baker's labour hard? Is not a baker worthy of the same respect as other tradesmen? Is not the labourer worthy of his hire? All he asks for is justice and fair play between capital and labour. Remember the determined attitude and success of the bakers in 1846 ; what they have done once they can do again. Then their cry was "No Surrender!"—their cry has not changed! Meet them in a liberal spirit and there will be no cause for regret.

Another great evil in Glasgow is the halflin question; and the great army of jobbers Glasgow is obliged to keep is another detriment to the trade. So much for the condition of the journeymen bakers in Glasgow. When some of the craft are seen to go astray, let us lead them with a kind word into better paths, thinking of Burns's "Address to the Unco, Guid," or Rigidly Righteous. I will quote the first and penultimate verses only:—

> "Oh ye wha are sae guid yoursel',
>   Sae pious an' sae holy,
> Ye've nought to do but mark an' tell
>   Your neebour's fauts an' folly!
> Whase life is like a weel gaun mill,
>   Supplied wi' store o' water,
> The heaped happer's ebbing still,
>   An' still the clap plays clatter.
>
> Then gently scan your brother man,
>   Still gentler sister woman ;
> Though they may gang a kennin' wrang
>   To step aside is human :
> One point must still be greatly dark
>   The moving why they do it :
> An' just as lamely can ye mark,
>   How far perhaps they rue it.'

FEDERATION.

"When the war-drum throbs no longer, and the battle-flags are furled,
In the parliament of man—the federation of the world."

There are supposed to be at the present time 4,500 master bakers—or rather employers; and 13,500 journeymen bakers in London; and in the United Kingdom, roughly speaking, say, 100,000. I am a supporter of federation, and would do my utmost to try and bring to a successful issue between England, Scotland, America, and Australia the amalgamation and unity of each association, so that a card of membership could readily be exchanged in each respective country.

This bond of brotherhood and union would, I am inclined to think, greatly help the journeyman bakers to make a better stand and take a higher platform than that they at present occupy. And such a union between employers of labour would have its corresponding advantages as well.

STATISTICS OF AMERICAN AND CANADIAN BAKERS AND CONFECTIONERS.

The following is taken from the Chicago "Confectioner and Baker":—

The total number of master bakers and confectioners in the United States and Canada is 25,000, of which Canada contributes 1,827. In the United States, Pensylvania heads the list with 3,000; New York, 2,550; Illinois, 2,000; Ohio, 1,400; Massachussets, 1,100; Missouri, 1,100; New Jersey, 1,000; Indiana, 850; Michigan, 800; Iowa (average) 750; Kansas, 750 Minnesota, 750; Winconsin, 750; Maryland, 575; Colorado, 475; Kentucky, 475; Nebraska, 400; Texas, 400 Arkansas, 400; Rhode Island, Tennessee, Vermont, Virginia and West

Virginia, from 250 to 800 each; other States, 2,273. Total in the United States, 23,173.

According to the above figures—and we have no reason to doubt them—the baking and confectionery trade in America is in a very flourishing condition.

INEFFICIENT WORKMEN.

> " Honour and shame from no condition rise :
> Act well your part ; there all the honour lies."—*Pope.*

This is a very delicate subject to meddle with, therefore I approach it with all due care. But it is, nevertheless, one of the burning questions that the baking trade, or the trade employers, will have at no very distant date to grapple with; and as I have passed through all the different grades of the trade, from apprentice boy to the proud position of master—or employer, as the word should be used—and am now working manager in a good-sized modern bakery, I claim to have a little knowledge of the requirements of the trade.

In the first place, what constitutes a baker ? I mean a skilful baker ; a man of some use in a trade that is amongst the largest—if not *the* largest, directly or indirectly—in existence. What I should call a baker is a man who, to begin with, has capabilities of ordinary calibre, has intuition, and a fair education; a man who starts as tin-boy, and goes through all the different grades till his time is properly served; not running from this employer to that in the hope of securing an extra shilling or two ; but a man who has served a proper and full apprenticeship, and stands in the proud position of being able to say that he is a properly-qualified journeyman baker. It has been my misfortune to have mixed with unqualified men; and I say, " Yeast and flour may to a certain extent be controlled ; but inefficient workmen, *never !* "

Bakers are not like other workmen, who can throw down their tools and leave at a moment's notice, without in any way interfering with the quality of their work; a baker has a living mass to contend with, as soon as, or shortly after his sponge is set, and he must carry it through its different stages, till placed before the public in a tradesmanlike manner. A warm oven, a strong sponge, bad yeast, and many other adverse things stare him in the face, but if he had an efficient staff of workmen, these things would to a great extent be prevented. Some may say, why not get a reference with a workman? I have done so. A short time since I had occasion to engage a man for a responsible position in the bakery; a reference was sent something after this style :—" This is to certify that the bearer has been in our employ for the last six years, and we can thoroughly recommend him as a good bread baker, and a capital hand amongst small goods and flour confectionery." Well, on the strength of his reference he got the place. The day after he came, orders were given as to what each had to do after the batches were out. I came up to this particular person, and asked him to get up a mixture of Madeira cakes; his answer was that he knew nothing whatever about confectionery. I drew his attention to his reference. " Well," quoth he," I can assist." " In what way ? " He said, " I can paper the hoops ! " Well, I was in a fog ! If he were discharged we might get no better; and, as it was a busy season, he was kept on at some 6s. or 8s. more a week than the next best man, who was a qualified baker and confectioner. Employers giving such references are guilty of a grave misdemeanour, and are no friends to the trade.

Cheap men, too, are another drawback. An employer dealing in cheap commodities finds himself as a rule in the bankruptcy court. A good man can always command a good wage. I would propose to obviate this difficulty by a training school;

and by making it compulsory for each baker to go through certain training, and gaining a certain certificate before being qualified to take a baker's situation. I think this plan on a sound basis would work well. Another nuisance is the rigidly righteous man, who will do his work and no more; and if asked to hurry up will say he is doing a fair day's work for a fair day's pay.

That there is a goodly sprinkling of useful, skilful men in the baking trade, the abundance of good bread made, and the successful competitions of British bakers at exhibitions, both at home and abroad, will amply testify. I consider every skilful practical baker who receives a thorough technical training, a valuable acquisition to the trade. But I am speaking of inefficient workmen—men whom all managers or foremen have to contend with. This inefficiency, as I said before, could be greatly avoided if we had our trade better organised.

Let us now turn to a more cheerful subject.

OLD CUSTOMS OF THE TRADE.

There is an old saying that old customs die hard; but there are one or two customs we would like to give more longevity to than they are likely to have, *viz.*, the yearly reunions of the trade; such as balls, suppers, and excursions, or, as they are called in London, "Bean Feasts." I can well remember my *debut* at a ball. As officer, that is, the oldest apprentice at the trade who had not held the office before, I was presented with a free ticket; the duties were not very onerous—just to deliver summonses, attend meetings, etc. At that particular ball, I can well remember many master bakers and master millers (as the millers and sugar boilers were counted with our craft), and how sociably the employers mixed with the employed; for a few weeks before, and a few weeks after, it helped to brighten the lives of the bakers, both young and old. The usual thing was for a young man to select a suitable partner, one who could dance of course; and on presenting her with a ticket, it was customary to present her with a pair of gloves, or the equivalent, say, from 5s. to 10s. according to his position. When the ball night (generally early in the new year) arrived, he would take a cab and call for his partner. Arrived safely, he would conduct her to the cloak-room, and next to the ball-room, where the ladies sat on one side and the gentlemen on the other. When all the guests arrived a slight refreshment would be served round. I have been one of the stewards, and it was pleasant to carry round a tray of eatables, or wine, etc., and chat with the ladies. Then the band would strike up the Grand March, and each baker and his partner walked round the room, the ball committee going in front. We always broke up the proceedings with regret, at about five o'clock in the morning; escorted our partners home, changed, and started our day's work and duties again. Bakers' suppers have given place to balls, and they seem to be dying out. I am alluding principally to provincial towns. The bakers used to club together to the tune of thirty or forty—though I have seen fewer. It used to be two shillings and sixpence per head; and subscriptions or collections were taken for the waiters or waitresses, and as a rule they used to fare very well. After all had gathered a chairman and vice-chairman were selected; then the landlord or lady was desired to bring in the good things provided for us—for the supper was usually held in an hotel. After someone had been asked to pronounce a blessing, the fun of the evening began. Ample justice being done to the viands, everything was cleared away, and refreshments came in the shape of cigars, pipes, and ale and whiskey, and the evening was enlivened with songs, recitations, etc., so that in an hour or two we could say with Burns—with a slight alteration—"Kings may be blest, but the bakers were glorious." The hotel proprietors were sometimes granted an extra hour, and the party broke up singing "Auld Lang Syne." At one of these reunions there was a baker, an old man, but one of the right sort, who could tell a good story and was generally put down for two or three songs after the supper—which songs always had a chorus, in which we all joined and made the rafters sound! They were mostly trade songs, and his refrains usually ran after this fashion:

"Every man to me's a brother
That wears flour upon his coat."

Or,—

"Bakers get enough to vex them,
Whiles wi' barm, an' whiles wi' flour."

The poor old man lived to a ripe old age, but has by this time crossed the bourn, and has known the grand Secret for some years.

Excursions are mostly the fashion now; and, of course, they will run till, as other fads are adopted, they become things of the past.

There used to be old customs of initiating a new apprentice into the mysteries of the trade. One was to get a new apprentice to go to a neighbouring bakery with an empty sack and ask for the loan of their crystal chaffer. When the boy arrived with his request he was asked to leave his sack and call in a few minutes, which he invariably did. In his absence all the available bricks and ashes were put into the sack, and a load made ready for him sufficient for a donkey to carry. When he arrived the crystal chaffer was lifted on to his back with strict injunctions not to let it fall, and the poor fellow had to manage as well as he could. But he was not likely to forget that journey, nor the laughter that greeted him on his return.

Another custom was to send a boy with a large pail for a pennyworth of pie-barm. He was, of course, asked to leave the pail, and bricks were put into the bottom of it, and it was filled up with water to the brim, with just a sprinkling of flour on the top. He was told not to spill any, as it was valuable and scarce. He generally managed to take it to the bakehouse, where the men laughed "fit to split" at his wrestling exertions to keep it from spilling.

Some eighteen months ago a new boy was engaged in our establishment, and in the first week I noticed on a particular day some of the men coming down the bakehouse stairs laughing, and others trying to suppress their mirth. I went upstairs to ascertain the cause, and on going into a certain place where the muffin stove is kept, whom should I see but the new apprentice trying to keep his hands in a tin of boiling fat, with the perspiration running down his face, and his body trembling all over. I asked him what was the matter. " I am boiling my hands, sir," said he, " so that the dough may not stick. If you please, sir, will you look at them and see if they will do ?" The poor boy's hands were in a bad state, and I gave an affirmative decision; but, though sorry for him, I nearly hurt myself with laughter, as though I had often heard of it I had never seen the trick played before.

Another old custom, but one which is rapidly becoming extinct, owing to the adoption of Parisian and other barms, was hunting for "skeechan" on a Sunday morning.* Not so many years ago Company's barm was used in many parts of Scotland, the chief seat of its manufacture being Edinburgh and Leith.

---

* This term must have been peculiar to the trade in certain districts, as I cannot find it in Jamieson's Scottish Dictionary. I have therefore given it so as to represent as nearly as possible the pronunciation common in the trade.

This barm in its constituent parts resembles brewers' barm, and was used in ferments much in the same way. There was a liquid that settled on the top of the barm, which was, compared to ale, what methylated spirit is to whiskey. This was the "skeechan." After a Saturday night's debauch, when the funds were low, it was a common custom for bakers to watch the time that the foreman went to set his ferment, so as to get a pint or two of this hateful concoction. Their *modus operandi* was to warm the liquid and sweeten it with sugar; and I have heard keen expressions of delight and approval from the partakers of this detestable beverage. But the majority of these poor, infatuated fellow-workmen gradually descended in their social position, till they reached that unenviable part of the community, the "submerged tenth." This old custom is, let us hope, a thing of the past.

Just another custom that used to exist in Scotland. At New Year's time a great quantity of shortbread was baked for the coming festivities, and the apprentice was allowed the scrapings. The shortbread, be it remarked, was scraped on the bottom before being sent into the shop. The apprentice was generally equal to the occasion, and made it known outside that he had shortbread scrapings for sale, a big handful for a half-penny. If trade was good, and the demand bade fair to be more than the supply, he used to mix bread raspings with the scrapings, which were often adulterated to such an extent as to spoil the custom.

A CANNY SCOT.

It is surprising and amusing to learn what ignorance was displayed by bakers at no very distant date in regard to the practical knowledge of working sponges. I could enumerate many instances, but this will suffice :—In a small town in Scotland a baker had just finished setting his ferment, when he heard the sound of a horse and cart coming into the street. He was afraid that the rattling of the cart would injure his ferment, and was greatly annoyed; so calling to the boy, said—" Rin awa, laddie, an' tell that chiel tae be canny wi' his cart ; I hae jist gat the ferment set." This individual would stare if he was brought into some of our modern bakeries, where there are ferments, quarter sponges, etc., all in different stages of operation, and machinery rattling loudly enough, one would think, to shake this Rip Van Winkle out of his bed.

SCIENTIFIC VIEWS ON FERMENTATIVE PHYSIOLOGY.

In order to further enhance the value of this work, and to keep the trade well to the front on this important subject, I have here introduced the opinions of a few leading British and Continental scientists on fermentation and fermentative physiology.

In an article on "Yeast—Its Morphology and Culture," A. Gordon Salamon, A.R.S.M., F.J.C., F.C.S., says :

" It remains, therefore, to decide as to whether it is an animal or a plant. In this we are again assisted by reference to the typical conditions pertaining to the life of both. Now microscopic examination of a yeast cell shows that it is surrounded by an envelope or sac of cellulose, and although there may be variations in the thickness of this envelope, there is reason to believe that it is continuous ; in other words, that it does not exhibit orifices such as exist in animals for the introduction of food within the system, and for the excretion of products voided as the result of food assimilation ; and further, since the single cell is capable of life and reproduction, it follows that the continuous cell wall and the contents which it encloses must constitute the whole machinery which is enabled to manifest these phenomena.

I

"In the case of nearly all animals the food is conveyed into the system by means of an opening adapted to the purpose. Now with the yeast cell such a means of introduction is impossible, because of the existence of the continuous cell wall, which is unprovided with openings; and if the cellulose wall were broken, the life of the cell would be determined. It is therefore clear that the only way in which food can be conveyed into the interior of the cell is by passage through the cellulose. This is, indeed, what actually happens, and it is accomplished by means of diffusion or osmosis. We shall inquire further into the nature of this process at a later stage; for the present it will suffice to state that one of the conditions essential to diffusion through cellulose is that the substance diffused must be in a state of solution; hence it follows that no food can be assimilated by yeast unless it is previously dissolved.

"These facts tend to prove that yeast is a plant, because a cellulose wall, and the passage of dissolved nutrient matter through it by osmosis, constitute two of the most essential conditions of plant life. But the conclusion is greatly strengthened, indeed corroborated, by other considerations dependent upon the chemical constitution of the food assimilated. Now animals and plants have this in common; apart from certain mineral elements, which, for the moment, we can ignore, they both require a supply, in some form or other, of the elements carbon, hydrogen, oxygen, and nitrogen. So, as far as information goes, these elements must be aggregated as certain molecular combinations before they can be regarded as nutrifying ingredients.

"Among these combinations we recognise a group of complex nitrogenous bodies known as proteins. Their supply would seem to be essential to a normal, healthy, and continued existence both of animals and plants. Suitable animal food contains these protein bodies ready formed in a state available for assimilation, and proportioned in quantity to the climatic conditions and life history of the organisms by which they are consumed. If the animal did not find the protein nourishment ready made it would not be competent for it to manfacture it or build it up out of the elements of which it is composed. For instance, protein bodies are strictly organic compounds as distinguished from minerals, and it would not be possible for any animal to form protein out of mineral matters. This is not so with plants. They are possessed of the property of forming or manufacturing it from the elements or from true mineral substances, which latter they have the power of breaking down or decomposing in order that the requisite elements may be devoted to the purpose. This is found to hold good with all plants, but with no animals; and it therefore establishes a fundamental difference between the two which is sufficient to constitute a reliable test in case of doubt. Applying it in our own case, we find that yeast is possessed of this power of forming protein out of mineral substances. The point has been abundantly proved by Pasteur. He showed how millions of cells, each containing its requisite amount of protein, could be produced in a healthy and thriving state from a smaller number of parent cells by introducing the latter into a fluid of the following definite composition: Water, sugar, ammonic tartrate, potassium phosphate, calcium phosphate, magnesium sulphate.

"The growth of yeast in this fluid is accompanied by the gradual disappearance of the above-named constituents, and the formation in all the newly-developed yeast cells of protein bodies. The latter were obviously not present in the original fluid. It can be proved that the mineral substances present have not the power of forming them in the absence of the yeast or some other similarly constituted organism, and hence it follows that in this case they must have been formed by the yeast, and at the expense of the original constituents of the fluid. Moreover, the recent researches of Hansen have shown that the same results could have been produced by introducing a single cell into the fluid instead of several or many, as was done by Pasteur."

Another high authority, William Jago, F.C.S., F.I.C., in the journal of the Society of Chemical Industry, thus treats on "Fermentation in its Relation to Bread Making":

"Fermentation has been made the subject of careful and systematic study in connection with brewing and the production of alcoholic liquors generally; but in its relation to bread-making has hitherto received but comparatively little attention from scientists. In many cases it has apparently been assumed that yeast behaves in just the same manner in dough as it does in a malt or other wort, and, consequently, that the same laws apply with equal force to the phenomena of fermentation in either substance. But the fermentation of wort differs from that of dough in several most important particulars. The former is a liquid, rich in maltose, and well adapted for the sustenance and growth of yeast; the latter is a stiff, elastic, semi-solid mass, containing but little readily fermentable matter. In wort, by a process of budding, yeast rapidly multiplies; but when added to dough the yeast cells show no signs of any reproduction by budding, but, on the contrary, gradually disappear, owing to the breaking down of the cell-walls. In the fermentation of wort but a small proportion of the effect is due to the yeast originally added, the greater part being produced by the new yeast cells formed as the progeny of those first introduced; but in dough the whole of the work is thrown on the yeast cells primarily introduced into the mass. These are so unfavourably situated as to have little or no power of reproduction, and consequently on their activity and vitality successful fermentation must depend. This being the case, it is evident that mature and vigorous yeast is more absolutely essential to the baker than even to the brewer; since, if the latter's initial fermentation be sluggish, the progeny of new cells may fairly be expected to be more active. On the other hand, absolute freedom from foreign ferments is not a point of such vital importance to the baker as to the brewer. In many cases, a yeast that on microscopic examination would be immediately rejected by the brewer, would be found capable of making good bread. I might even go a step further and say that of two yeasts the one deemed the better of the two, judging by purity as revealed by the microscope, might be the less desirable yeast for bread-making purposes. It is a well-recognised fact that in some varieties of bakers' barms the presence of other organisms than the yeast plant is normal. In particular, this is so with Scotch flour barms, which consist of yeast allowed to develop in what is essentially a thin paste made from scalded flour. This barm invariably contains the lactic ferment in large numbers.

"Theory and practice both show that the aeration of the dough is only one out of several important effects produced by fermentation. From time to time, those interested in other methods of bread manufacture insist on the great loss caused by fermentation; thus, Dauglish expressed the opinion that this loss amounted to from 3 to 6 per cent., which opinion has since been adopted by Dr. Richardson in his work on the "Healthy Manufacture of Bread." In order to determine the maximum amount of loss possible, I recently made the following experiment: 100 parts by weight of soft flour from English wheats were made into a slack dough with distilled water, two parts of pressed yeast being added, and no salt used. This dough was allowed to stand for from eight to nine hours at a temperature of about 85° to 90° F.; fermentation proceeded violently, but towards the end of the time had apparently ceased. The dough was next placed in the hot-water oven, and dried until of constant weight;

the same weight of flour and yeast, unmixed, and without water, was also placed in the oven. At the end of the time, the fermented dough was found to have lost 2·5 per cent. compared with the flour. In this extreme case, a soft flour was used with distilled water and no salt, and about six times the normal amount of yeast; the temperature was purposely maintained at a high point, and the fermentation carried on so long as any decided evolution of gas occurred. Yet, under these conditions, which far and away exceed in severity any such as occur in practice, the loss was less than Dauglish's minimum estimate. The percentage of loss closely corresponds with that of sugar in flour as determined in a series of experiments to which I wish to direct your attention. Mr. Williams, a practical baker of high authority, estimates, from a series of experiments he conducted on a large scale, that the loss of solid constituents of flour during fermentation, as practically conducted in bakeries, amounts to 1·37 per cent."

Mr. Thoms, F.R.M.S., a Scotch master-baker, who has for very many years investigated yeast most exhaustively from the baker's standpoint, is the authority for the following. He says:

" On brewing flour-barm at a sufficiently low temperature to prevent the development of *Bacterium Lactis*, the barm produced is inferior in quality and yields an inferior loaf. It should be added that in bread made on the Scotch system there is always a distinct, though very slight acid flavour; this acidity is altogether different in character from what is known as sourness in bread in the London district. The flavour of Scotch bread more resembles that wetted partly with buttermilk. With healthy, active yeast cells, fermentation, as conducted in the south, proceeds sufficiently rapidly in dough to allow the bread to be completely ready for the oven before the lactic ferments have had time to develop any sensible acidity. In deciding as to the quality of yeast for bread-making purposes the first requisite is that the yeast plant itself should be in a vigorous and active condition. Among foreign ferments the presence of those producing lactic, at least, is not deleterious in small numbers to anything like the extent that holds in the case of yeast to be used for beer brewing. Apart from their own specific action, foreign ferments are, in brewer's yeast, an evidence of carelessness and want of strict cleanliness in the yeast manufacture, and to this extent their presence may be interpreted unfavourably when judging the value of such a yeast for the baker. The thing I hope I have made clear is, that if the yeast itself is healthy and vigorous, foreign ferments are not capable of doing the same amount of harm during the fermentation of dough, as during that of beer, principally because the act of baking the bread effectually destroys all fermentative action before disease ferments have had time to set up any injurious chemical change. In passing, the aim of the baker in availing himself of the action of the yeast during bread-making may be explained. If the question were asked, ' Why is yeast employed ?' the answer in ninety-nine cases out of a hundred would be—' To aerate the dough, and thus make the bread spongy.' Now yeast possesses this property in common with various other substances. There are, in fact, several ways of aerating bread more or less satisfactorily, but fermentation seems to be the only method capable of inducing other changes which are essential to the production of bread of the finest quality. By the action of yeast, the gluten, which contains the principal nitrogenous constituents of flour, is softened and mellowed, undergoing a species of digestive action, partly physical, inasmuch as it is rendered softer; and probably partly chemical, as a change analogous to peptonisation apparently occurs. Another most interesting effect of fermentation is that it imparts a characteristic and pleasant flavour to bread absolutely unattainable by other means. In bread aerated by any other method, the result of these specific changes is absent; and public opinion decides that, after a time, such bread raised otherwise than by the action of yeast has a raw uncooked taste, of which the palate speedily tires. Although the average baker knows nothing of the nature of the chemical changes induced by yeast, it is of great interest to note that his methods take cognisance of the fact that such changes are produced. If the production of sufficient gas to aerate the dough were his only object, then it might be expected that as soon as that object was attained, he would proceed to get his bread in the oven. Such, however, is not the case. After a time, as much as possible of the gas generated in the dough is violently knocked out of it, this operation being sometimes repeated two or three times. The baker knows by experience that other changes which he desires to have take place, will not be completed until some time after sufficient gas to aerate the bread has been developed. Theory and practice, therefore, both show that the aeration of the dough is only one out of several important effects produced by fermentation."

Dr. Emil Chr. Hansen, in a series of papers on "Practical Researches in Fermentation," thus gives the practical results obtained by the use of pure cultivated yeasts—of which he was one of the first advocates :—

"When, in 1883, I asked permission of the late Captain Jacobsen to try my system on a large scale at his brewery at 'Old Carlsberg,' he did not give me much encouragement. One of his principal objections was that a pure cultivated yeast would not ensure proper after-fermentations, to which an admixture of wild types was probably essential. Shortly before I had obtained some remarkable practical results, tending strongly to confirm the correctness of my views of Saccharomycetes. In a paper on 'Diseases of Beer' (*Compte-rendu du Laboratoire de Carlsberg*,

1883), I explained the affection which for two years past had proved so troublesome at the Tuborg brewery, near Copenhagen —*i.e.*, yeast-turbidity, and as application of my conclusions had speedily put matters right, manifest proof was afforded of the practical worth of my discoveries. About the same time Jacobsen experienced a difficulty in his own brewery, where the beer had acquired a bitter twang and a bad smell. According to the then prevailing idea, this was attributed to bacterial infection, and when this could not be detected, the blame was laid on the wort and more particularly on the hops. Here, likewise, nothing could be detected. Previously, in 1882, I had published an account of an experiment with one of the saccharomycetes, which gave a beer similar to that complained of at Old Carlsberg. I also mooted the idea that wild yeasts do as much mischief in various departments of fermentative industry as bacteria. In 1883 I advanced a step further. My success at Tuborg afforded me the desired opportunity. This experiment was carried out in actual brewing practice, on a large scale, and the proofs obtained step by step were irrefragable. From an impure yeast I separated four different types of saccharomycetes, and after experimenting with them singly and in admixture, found that only one of them gave normal beer of good flavour and smell. Among the others I found the type I had employed in my experiment of 1882, and of which I gave a description in 1883, under its present name of *Saccharomyces pastorianus I.* This alone produced the affections in question. Further, I found that whilst beer produced with the suitable type of yeast alone was excellent, the admixture of *Saccharomyces pastorianus I* therewith gave the dreaded bitter taste and disagreeable smell. This result proved of great importance. Jacobsen saw that reform was practically within reach, and threw open his whole establishment for the purpose. A beginning thus made, matters progressed as rapidly as ever I could desire. That was in 1884. I have mentioned the results obtained in the two breweries just named, partly to show the progressive development of the idea, partly as affording tangible proofs in favour of a reform which I desired to see spread as widely as possible. Proof was likewise afforded that Jacobsen's fears respecting after-fermentation were groundless. Nevertheless, the doubt has since been raised in other quarters (see Brown and Morris's paper on 'The Non-Crystallisable Products of the Action of Diastase on Starch' in *Journal of the Chem. Soc.*, 1885.) Among English experimenters only, I have met with the objection that the highly alcoholic English top-fermentation beers present special difficulties in the way of employing pure cultures. In Danish top-fermentation breweries, where less alcoholic beers are produced without special after-fermentations, A. Jörgensen has since 1884 employed the method, slightly modified, with satisfactory results, and in accordance with his verbal explanations, the principle has been lately adopted in a few foreign breweries worked on the same lines as the English. To the weight of Jacobsen's authority I owe it that my practical experiments became so soon known in my own land as well as in other countries. Most of them, however, were and are still received by intelligent brewers with distrust. This opposition would have further retarded the adoption of the idea, but for the stout support it has received from Aubry from the very outset. To him belongs the credit of having introduced this reform into Germany. In Bohemia, Bêlohoubek, and in Norway, Hejberg have made a beginning. Here in Denmark my efforts have been supported by A. Jörgensen and Grünlund. In Jörgensen's laboratory there has been great activity. Not only the numerous breweries in Scandinavia, but most of those in other countries have received their supplies of pure yeast therefrom. In France,

Louis Marx has taken up the idea, which but for him would there have scarce borne fruit. Among foreign chemists and botanists who have studied with me, I have found many active co-operators.

"The brewery at Old Carlsberg, since the year 1884, and likewise that of New Carlsberg and others, depend entirely on my supplies of pure cultivated yeasts. The fermenting vats at Old Carlsberg contain 9,000 hect. (198,000 galls.) of wort, and the yeast employed in pitching amounts to 2,500 kilogs. (50 cwt.). Therewith are produced every year 200,000 hect. (122,000 barrels) of lager and export beer. The production at New Carlsberg is very little less. The aggregate value is many millions of marks. The greater part of all this beer is brewed with one species of yeast, that known as Carlsberg bottom-yeast No. 1; the small remaining portion is brewed with another pure cultivated species, that known as Carlsberg bottom-yeast No. 2. I mention these figures to show that we are not dealing with experiments on a small scale, but with solid results in an industry of great magnitude. Glancing at the progress of the reform, we see that it has now found its way into nearly all beer-producing countries. In Denmark and Norway it is now adopted in all the largest breweries. In Sweden a beginning has been made; likewise in Finland, in Bohemia and other parts of the Austrian domains; in Switzerland, North Italy, Belgium, and North America. We find it generally adopted, and established on a solid practical basis in Denmark and Norway, also in Russia, Holland, and Germany, particularly Bavaria. From Old Carlsberg supplies of pure yeast have been sent to breweries in Asia, and from Jörgensen's laboratory to Asia, Australia, and South America. Whether the method has taken root in these remote countries, I am unable to state. What has just been said shows clearly that the system offers certain advantages. Examined more closely, there will be found to be:—1—That a definite result is assured by determinate means; whereas previously all was problematical. 2—That security is afforded against diseases in beer, which entail serious loss. 3—That a yeast is thus obtained which fetches a higher price in the trade than ordinary impure yeast. 4—That a new development is thus given to industrial production—a consideration of moment to all practical men."

I think I have now sufficiently shown how scientists are step by step working out a great change in our opinions respecting fermentation, and daily adding to our knowledge of its varied properties.

THE PROPERTIES OF STARCH.

Starch is a food which is largely required to sustain the human system; it is supplied abundantly in all "farinaceous" substances (the word merely meaning "starchy"), such as arrowroot, sago, tapioca, semolina, etc. Arrowroot is prepared from the root stocks of several East and West Indian plants. Sago is also prepared from a deposit in the trunks of several species of palms. Tapioca is got from the roots of the passava tree; but semolina is made from wheat, and, in addition, contains a certain proportion of albuminous gluten; it is therefore more nourishing as a food than any of the above. The three first-named substances are nearly pure starch, when they are unadulterated. But starch is found in one form or other, and in some quantity or other, in nearly all plants. Starch, when seen by the naked eye, is a white, glistening powder, but when viewed through a miscroscope, it appears like a series of very small semi-transparent grains, of sizes which vary according to the origin of the starch—in some cases they are so minute as the ten-thousandth part of an inch in diameter. The shape of the grain is very irregular, but the different kinds are readily known to a practised eye, the starch from wheat, for example, being different in size and general appearance to that derived from potatoes. Starch is composed of carbon, hydrogen, and oxygen, which enter into its composition always in the same proportions, no matter how the grains may differ in size and appearance. Starch in itself is insoluble, but it is readily changed into a soluble gum called dextrine, and also, by the addition of water, into glucose or sugar. Should anyone wish to extract natural starch from vegetables, let him pound a raw potato in water, and pass it through a fine hair sieve, which will remove the tissue and fibre ; then allow the liquid which passes through the sieve to remain until all the starch it carries settles, when the water can be poured off, and pure starch will remain.

DRYNESS OF BREAD MADE FROM ROLLER-GROUND FLOUR.

Ever since the introduction of rollers for milling or grinding wheat into flour, the want of moisture in bread has been a vexed question, and not without cause. The upholders of roller-ground flour may rant and rave, and quote statistics to prove their theory that the bread made from it is equally as moist as flour milled in the old system, *viz.*, stone-ground flour. But still the fact remains that, since the introduction of roller-ground flour, bread is drier, has less keeping qualities, and gives a poorer " yield " per sack than stone-ground flour. So if this is *not* the cause of the husky dryness in bread noticeable of recent years, what may it be? This may appear to some to be begging the question, but I cannot perceive a better way of sustaining my argument. We are supposed to have better yeast with all the latest chemical improvements—likewise better ovens, with steam generators to ensure moisture, but the dry huskiness still remains. Many a hot argument have I had on this question with men whom one would have thought capable of knowing better. Men who are interested in the manufacture and sale of this particular flour must necessarily put it before the trade in as gilded colours as possible, but say what they will the dryness is still there. I do not for a moment doubt its fine, mellow tint, nor deny that it looks more enticing, and richer to the eye and judgment of purchasers of this commodity, but, as I have said, the dry huskiness remains. For biscuit flour I much prefer it to stone-ground flour, but for batch bread I would not commend it for moisture, general appearance, and yielding powers. I hope no one will accuse me of taking too pessimistic a view of this question, as I believe that the border of it only has been touched. I likewise sincerely believe that there are men capable of overcoming this grave difficulty of the dryness in roller-ground flour—and that in the near future. Now since its cause has been ascertained, and every cause has its corresponding effect, let the effect be removed and the cause will cease. In regard to this question an eminent authority in Paris—M. Lucas, director of the flour market—has recently made a discovery which is of great importance in dealing with it. What, asks M. Lucas, is the cause of roller flour drying out, and being less savoury than burr flour? To this question he gives a plain decisive answer. The baking quality of flour depends chiefly on the oil contained in the germs of the grain. Now, by the roller process, these germs, and along with them the oily matter, are separated from the flour, while they are retained in the burr flour. Hence the better taste and softness of bread made of the latter, which, however, has one defect—the oil retained in it is greatly oxidisable, causing the flour to spoil in a very short time, a circumstance impossible in the former, being devoid of oily matter. Now, as we have found the effect, is there any remedy? M. Lucas says there is. Aimé Girard has found that the quantity of the oil eliminated from the flour by the roller process is 0·210 per cent. of the flour's weight. From this knowledge M. Lucas infers that a proper substitute for the oil extracted by this process will give the bread made from roller flour the same baking quality as is possessed by the burr flour. Experiments enabled him to discover that the oil of sweet almonds contains all the qualities necessary to produce the desired result. Almond oil mixed with the dough in the ratio of 2 grammes to 1 kilogramme, produced a bread not only just as savoury and elastic as the burr flour bread, but even superior to it, which M. Lucas explains from the fact that the roller flour is not liable to become sour, while the other does after a time. On the other hand, bread made of the same kind of flour without the addition of almond oil invariably proved tasteless and dried out very soon. This experiment was repeated a good many times, and the results submitted to the judgment of experts, who at once and always discovered the difference of the two kinds of bread as to taste and softness, but were at a loss to account for the cause. So the above discovery will be of the greatest importance to all interested in the flour and bread trade.

Thus we have Science and Art marching side by side (or at least, the little science that we can put to practical use in the baking trade). The abridged extracts from a recent writer on the colour and chemical examination of flour given in a preceding chapter, and the above article on the dryness of roller-ground flour, taken in conjunction with the practical knowledge I have given in this work, will, I trust, help the bread-baker to more fully understand the varied methods recently adopted in modern flour milling.

THE CAUSES OF HOLES IN BREAD.

Why bread should be holey, is a question more readily asked than answered. The holes occur in different parts of the loaf, being sometimes between the crumby part and the bottom part of the top crust, and sometimes altogether in the crumby part. In either case the causes are different. One of the primary causes is improper workmanship—such as making the dough, either by hand or machine, in a happy-go-lucky manner; working against time, etc., etc. Scrappy or undermade dough offers less resistance to the accumulated gas, which will follow the track of least resistance more readily than it will follow or force a passage through the better made portion of the dough. Bad moulding is another cause. Let any practical man mould some dough in a soft, flabby manner, and bake a loaf along with his ordinary batch in an oven of extreme heat, and the chances are it will have a hollow, or snuff-box top, and will cut holey all through. I have likewise noticed that a small quantity of bread baked in an oven heated to receive its full complement, with the oven-door open, tends to become holey. Under-proved bread also tends to this result, and should be avoided. Strong yeasts have been erroneously credited with causing holes in bread; I, for one, am inclined to question the truth of this. Weak yeasts cause holes, but not so strong yeasts. If a piece of dough is made without yeast, and baked in an ordinary oven, a certain quantity of holes will be found. This rather favours the opinion that weak yeasts, and not good strong ones, are to blame for the defect. If this virgin dough is placed in the oven the heat will cause steam to come from it during the process of baking. This steam, when it leaves the dough, leaves a vacancy behind it; if the dough had been properly manipulated, and assisted with healthy fermentation, no holes could occur. Or, to take another instance, *viz.*, home-made bread, when the housewife is short of the staff of life, she will invariably take a part of her sponge dough, mould it round, and pin it out the size of a large plate. She will then place it in the oven without any proof, and the result is heavy, sodden, and holey bread; which at once shows that the defects are due to weakness, as the gluten in this case has not been sufficiently decomposed.

Strong flour is sometimes blamed for causing holes in bread; but my experience contradicts this. In our establishment we are in the habit of using four different grades of flour daily. Our first quality—Hungarian—is a good, strong, rich flour, and bread made from this has no suspicion of the above complaint. Our next in quality is good, strong, double-superfine, and I have never noticed in this any tendency to holey bread. The next we employ is superfine, a strong flour, but darker in colour than either of the above grades: this likewise makes good bread without holes. We have another class, namely fine, weaker in strength and darker in colour than the above. I have sometimes seen bread from this flour inclined to be holey; but never in our strong flours. I may say that this complaint is almost extinct in our establishment.

Potatoes, when used in ferments, if of unsound condition, are likewise to blame for the above defect: for this the remedy at hand is their entire disuse.

But one of the most common causes is the excessive use of low-priced Indian wheat, now used by most millers in the production of cheap flours. This class of wheat is nearly devoid of gluten; and any practical baker knows that the amount of gluten in bread is shown by its rising qualities. The decomposition of gluten facilitates the fermenting qualities of the dough, therefore, no gluten means no rising power. In fermenting, this class of flour has a slow, deadened movement, and feels anything but lively. It also requires a longer time to prove, and when baked has little or no bloom. Extreme heat in the oven is necessary to produce anything approaching bloom on the top. Flour of this grade should be boycotted out of the British market; it is a worry to the journeyman, and a loss to the employer, besides giving but little satisfaction to the public who buy it.

These facts, then, seem to prove that weakness in flour or yeast, or feebleness of fermentative powers under any conditions, are more conducive to holes in bread than when the ingredients used are of a strong and healthy nature.

PERSONAL CLEANLINESS, ETC.

From a sanitary standpoint, I would suggest that it be made compulsory that all bakers, whether employers, managers, foremen, or journeymen, should undergo a periodical medical examination. There should be no exemption, wherever the parties here referred to are in the habit of manipulating bread, etc. If this proposition were put into force, and carried out as it ought to be, we should only be fulfilling a duty we owe to the public, as well as doing our utmost to prevent the spread of contagious diseases. The details for the above proposal could very simply be arranged for; but as the question at issue is a delicate one, let us for the present draw a veil, with the hope that the idea will only be the germ of a healthier future, both for bakers and our clients, the public. Do not let us be too thin-skinned, and plod on, content to live and work in the old-fashioned style, when we have modern science telling us the penalty we must pay for harbouring the microbes of disease. The necessities of the times demand a change.

On the other hand, we have employers who, as regards exterior appearances, are really too extreme. If they will only

modify their ideas as to how a workman should appear at work, the
"masher" baker will soon become a thing of the past. This
brings to my mind a story I once heard of a Glasgow employer
of this stamp. As the story goes, he advertised for a baker and
confectioner. A smart young fellow, who had had the misfortune
to be out of work for some time, and whose garments indicated
that he was in no way related to the dignified Beau Brumell
class, applied for the place. The employer critically eyed the
applicant all over, and said, "Well, my young man, if I offer
you the situation, I presume you will be able to come to your
work in a better suit of clothes than those you are at present
wearing, as I have rather a select trade." The astonished
young man looked at him, and said, "I beg your pardon, sir;
I was not aware that it was a suit of clothes you were advertising
for—I thought it was a baker."

AN APPEAL TO THE TRADE.

Unless a desperate effort be at once made to reconstruct the
present loose system of making bread, too often carried on in
some of our bakeries, the bulk of the bread trade is destined to
drift gradually into the hands of female bakers. Members of the
trade should not forget that gas and kitchen ovens are
getting pretty well perfected, and ovens of this class
are cheap and handy. Good yeast can also be had at a low
price. Indeed, yeast is at present retailed as one of our necessary
commodities in most provision shops in England. We, likewise,
are not ignorant of the fact that the female part of the community
has already laid the first plank in that platform which will soon
lift them above all forms and customs. Women, in general, are
quick in perception, and not very far behind men in reflective
powers. Let them once make a passable loaf, and the art of

baking becomes so fascinating that they often get baking on the brain. But I have seen bread made by the mother of a large family, that for flavour and colour would vie with that made by many of our so-called professional bread bakers. This is one of those practical facts that so many members of our craft "pooh-pooh," and try to shirk; but I can assure them that this is one of the leading forces that help to keep the baking trade from gaining that position it is so justly entitled to. It would be for the benefit of the trade to ponder over this, and not forget the old Scotch proverb that "a steek in time saves nine."

Another question which appeals very forcibly to everyone connected with the baking trade is that of a representative in Parliament. The mining, agricultural, and other industries are well represented; why, then, should we be exempt from sharing the benefits which are accorded to those whose professions require less skill, and whose responsibility to the masses is neither so far-reaching nor so closely connected with their welfare? If we had a trade representative in Parliament it would open up a new era in our trade, and be another instance of history repeating itself; for did not imperial Rome repeatedly accept and honour one or two of our craft in her dignified Senate?

CONCLUDING REMARKS.

Fellow-bakers and workers, do the right and help yourselves; let each one take his part for the advancement of our trade. If this be done as it ought to be done, and the results are not favourable to us as a body of tradesmen, I shall cry "Peccavi!" and at once humbly submit to correction. But I have confidence that through your energy, courage, and perseverance, a brighter and a better time is looming in the near future for the baking trade.

The so-called scientific baker has conjured up a monster that lies like an incubus on the trade; and this monster will have to take a more definite shape before practical bakers can accept its value, and assume a more prepossessing aspect before they can accept it as a practical or infallible guide. Scientific bread-baking exists more in anticipation than the reality. But when the science of our trade is so much in its infancy, what are really wanted at the present time are good practical men who can with favourable conditions produce favourable results.

My candid opinion on the art of good bread-making—after thirty years' practical experience—is that, with good yeast, good flour, water and salt, and with a systematic style of blending and manipulating the same, I will give my scientific opponents all the advertised nostrums and science they may have a mind to use, and be in no way afraid of the results.

INDEX.

Adulteration, 87
Aerated Bread, 54
   ,,   Malt Bread, 64
Alum, Potatoes, etc., 87
American and Canadian Bakers and Confectioners, Statistics of, 105
   ,,   Patent Yeast, 12
Appeal to the Trade, An, 131
Appendix, 94
Apple Bread, 67

Bakehouses, Ventilation of, 77
Bakers and Confectioners, Statistics of American and Canadian, 105
   ,,   in Glasgow, Journeyman, 102
   ,,   in London, Journeyman, 100
   ,,   in the time of the Romans, 94
Bakery, Utensils Required in a Modern, 83
Baking and Bakers in the time of the Romans, 94
Baps, 59
Barley Bread, 69
Barms, 6
Barm, Brewer's, 13 ; Malt and Hop, 10 ; Parisian, 7 ; Sour Parisian, 9 ; Store, 11 ; Virgin, 10
   ,,   On "Bringing Away," without any previously made being mixed with the freshly-made liquid, 9
Batch of Bread, How to Weigh-off a, 41
Batches, Setting or Running, 46
Boarding, 44
Box Rolls, 53
Bread, Aerated, 54 ; Apple, 67 ; Debretzen, 70 ; Germ, 65 ; Made from Roots, 67 ; Maslen, 63 ; Meslin, 68 ; Oat and Barley, 69 ; Patent or Unleavened, 55 ; Pulled, 54 ; Ragwort, 68 ; Rye, 62 ; Salep, 69 ; Soda, 54 ; Turnip, 68 ; Vienna, 50
Bread a Hundred Years Ago, 70
   ,,   A Standard for, 80

INDEX.

Bread, Causes of Holes in, 128
,, Home-made, 55 ; Home-made with Brewer's Barm, 56
,, made from Roller-ground Flour, Dryness of, 125
,, Old, How to Use up, 79
,, Plain and Fancy, 48
,, Sourness in, 29
,, Wheat-meal, 61 ; Substitutes for do., 66 ; Unfermented do., 65
Bread Tins, Seasoning, 79
Brewer's Barm, 13
,, ,, Home-made Bread from, 56
Brown Bread, Wheat Meal, Rye, etc., 59
Brown Bread Meal, 63

Canny Scot, A, 112
Carrying Flour, On, 81
Causes of Holes in Bread, 128
Chemical Examinations of Flour, 3
Cleanliness, Personal, 130
Cobs, 51
Coburgs, 51
Cold or Chilled Dough, Effects of, on the Heat of an Oven, 78
Compressed Yeast when Stale and Unfit for Use, 13
Concluding Remarks, 132
Cottage Loaves, 51
Customs of the Trade, Old, 103
Cutting Dough, Method of, 40

Debretzen Bread, 70
Diet, or Wheat-meal Bread, Unfermented, 65
Dough, The Manipulation of, 39
,, How to Make by Hand, 39
,, How to Roll-up Loaves of, 42
,, Method of Cutting, 40
Dryness of Bread made from Roller-ground Flour, 125

English Compressed Yeast, 14

Fancy Bread, 48
,, Cottage Loaves, 50
Federation, 105
Fermentation, 20
Fermentative Physiology, Scientific Views on, 113
Fermented Malt Bread, 64
Flour, 1

Flour, Chemical Examination of, 3
,,   Ferments, 33
,,   On Carrying, 81
,,   Spiced, 5
Flying Sponges, 37
Foreign Element in London, The, 99
French Loaves, 53
,,   Yeast, 14
Furnace Ovens, 74

General Details, 77
German Yeast, 13
Germ Bread, 65
Glasgow, Journeyman Bakers in, 102

Heating New Ovens, 79
Heat of Water, How to Ascertain the, 80
Holes in Bread, The Causes of, 128
Home-made Bread, 55
,,   ,, with Brewers' Barm, 56
Hot Rolls in England, 57

Inefficient Workmen, 107

Leaven, 17
Loaf, How to Mould a Square, 43
,,   How to Mould a Round, 44
Loaves—Common Vienna, 52 ; Fancy Cottage, 50 ; French, 53 : Melvin, 53 ; Sandwich, 53
,,   made in Britain, Names of various, 56
,,   of Dough, How to Roll-up, 42
London, Journeyman Bakers in, 100
,,   The Foreign Element in, 99

Machinery, Tools, etc., 82
Malt and Hop Barm, 10
Malt Bread—Aerated, 64 ; Fermented, 64
Manipulation of Dough, The, 39
Maslen Bread, 63
Meal, Brown Bread, 63
,,   Wheat, 59
Melvin Loaves, 52
Meslin Bread, 68
Modern Method of Sponging, 35

Moulding and Boarding, 44

Oat and Barley Bread, 69
Old Bread, How to Use up, 79
,, Customs of the Trade, 108
Ovens, 71
 ,, Furnace, 74 ; Scotch, 74 ; Waggon, 72 ; Various Other, 76
 ,, Heating New, 79
 ,, Effect of Cold or Chilled Dough on the heat of, 78
 ,, Overnight Sponging in large Firms, 37
Over-wrought Sponges, How to Treat, 38

Parisian Barm, 7
 ,, ,, Sour, 9
 ,, ,, To Make a Full Sponge with, without Quarter or Ferment, 37
Patent or Unleavened Bread, 55
Personal Cleanliness, etc., 130
Plain and Fancy Bread, etc., 48
Potatoes, etc., 87
Properties of Starch, The, 124
Pulled Bread, 54
Pyrometers, 83

Quarter Sponges to take up One Sack of Flour, 34
Quick or Flying Sponges, 37

Ragwort Bread, 68
Rolls, Box, 53 ; Scotch, 58
 ,, in England, Hot, 57
Romans, Baking and Bakers in the Time of the, 94
Roots, Bread Made from, 67
Round Loaf, How to Mould a, 44
Running Batches, 46
Rye, 59
 ,, Bread, 62

Salep Bread, 69
Salt, 18
Sandwich Loaves, 53
Scientific Views on Fermentative Physiology, 113
Scotch Ovens, 74
 ,, Rolls, 58
 ,, Yeast, 14

Seasoning Bread Tins, 79
Setting or Running Batches, 46
Soda Bread, 54
Sourness in Bread, 29
Sour Parisian Barm, 11
Spiced Flour, 5
Sponge, How to Set a, 37
,, To Make a Full, with Parisian Barm, Without Quarter or Ferment, 37
Sponges, On Increasing and Decreasing, 28
,, How to Treat Over-wrought, 38
,, Quarter, to Take up One Sack of Flour, 34
,, Quick or Flying, 37
,, Unripe, 32
Sponging, 26
,, Modern Method of, 35
,, in large Firms, Overnight, 37
,, Sunday, 26
Square Loaf, How to Mould a, 43
Standard for Bread, A, 80
Starch, The Properties of, 124
Store Barm, 11
Sunday Sponging, 26

Tools, etc., 82
Turnip Bread, 68
Twists, How to Make, 51

Unleavened Bread, 55
Unripe Sponges, 32
Utensils Required for a Modern Bakery, 83

Ventilation of Bakehouses, 77
Vienna Bread, 50
,, Loaves, Common, 52
Virgin Barm, 10

Waggon Ovens, 72
Water, 19
,, How to Ascertain the Heat of, 80
Wheat Bread, Substitutes for, 61
Wheat Meal, 59
,, ,, Bread, 61; Unfermented, 65

Yeast, American Patent, 12; English Compressed, 14; French, 14 ;
    German, 13 ; Scotch, 14
  ,, How to Keep Pure, 17
Yeasts and Barms, On, 6
  ,, Compressed, When Stale and Unfit for Use, 15

CPSIA information can be obtained
at www.ICGtesting.com
Printed in the USA
JSHW081305260123
36889JS00001B/37